HISTORY OF BAROQUE MUSIC

HISTORY OF BAROQUE MUSIC

by Kurt List

ORPHEUS / New York

Printed in the United States of America

PREFACE

Music of Western society has had one basic language for the past four hundred years. Yet only the works of the 120-year period dating roughly from the time of the twenty-year-old Mozart to that of Richard Strauss have become the mainstays of our concert halls and opera houses.

And what about the others? Composition after Richard Strauss is something our audiences approach with caution. The works of the two hundred years which preceded Mozart, with the possible exception of those by Bach and Handel, are heard only occasionally, and this despite a resurgence of interest in precisely that period of writing.

The layman (and very often the musician) is baffled by the variety of styles and their tentative attempts to create a new, universal body of music. Yet, the works of this pre-Mozart period are not only the foundation of all that is familiar in music today; they are, in many cases, masterpieces which need not fear comparison with those by Schumann, Liszt, Tchaikovsky, and many others of the standard concert fare.

Perhaps, the layman will establish more interest for, and a closer relationship to, this period by looking into its artistic motivation.

To this end, our project consisting of both text and music has been created. Possibly, it is more correct to call it a concert with explanatory footnotes and not a booklet with musical examples. If approached as such, it may open up a whole new world of fantastic musical sounds and shapes.

Brione sopra Minusio,
August 14, 1965

KURT LIST

I should like to express my gratitude to Miss Hilde Langfort for some valuable suggestions regarding the program material, to Dr. Helmut Riessberger for his assistance in research, and, above all, to Miss Dietlinde Hofmann for putting the manuscript into its final shape.

K. L.

CONTENTS

PART ONE

1

INTRODUCTION
Purpose and Intent

This book is not a history of music. Better accounts of musical events have been, and will be, written. Nor are musical happenings made to fit preconceived theories. Too many of these theories already clutter our minds. However, two, in particular, must invite closer inspection; they are the evolutionary and socio-historical standpoints.

The evolutionary view, if not interpreted in a biological sense, might give an approximation to truth. But associated with it is what e. e. cummings calls the comfortable disease—the idea of progress. Once one believes that a development tends toward a certain goal, he is also seduced into thinking that this goal is on a level higher than all that led to it. Undoubtedly, the technological evolution of music materials, such as instruments, makes for extensions affecting range and dynamics. But does it follow that *Der Rosenkavalier* is better music than *L'Incoronazione di Poppea?*

If we do not believe that the Pyramids are inferior to the architecture of Lincoln Center, we will not hold that qualitative adjectives can attach themselves to subsequent stages of artistic development. In short, the arts are not a series of advances.

On the other hand, every good artist bases his work on the achievements of his predecessors. It depends on his imagination and inventiveness as to what and how much from the preceding generations he uses, to what purpose he puts the thus absorbed material, and in which way he elaborates on and develops it. In this process he is as likely to take a step down as up, aesthetically speaking.

At each stage, man giving his best creates art; but at one stage man's best may be inferior to his best at another. It is supercilious for later generations to look at works of previous ages from the vantage point of superiority or even to try to "improve" on them. (This should caution us against some modern editions and transcriptions of older music.)

Although no all-encompassing theory can be built on the evolutionary view, it still is important enough to make us sort out various tendencies that lead to further achievements in subsequent periods. One need only guard against classifying them qualitatively rather than genetically.

If the evolutionary approach suffers from Candide's optimism, the socio-historical view is impeded by a sort of Hegelian mechanistic procedure. This involves interrelating historical, sociological, and artistic phenomena in such a manner as to suggest that simultaneous happenings could also establish a causal interaction.

Indisputably, social and material conditions influence the arts. In music, the nature of the composer's employment often determines the type of composition requested of him. The character of instrumentation follows from the number, species, and technological status of the instruments at hand which, in turn, depend on the social conditions under which the composer operates. The acoustics of the hall for which some works are written might guide their style in certain directions. But beyond this, to insinuate deeper and, indeed, sometimes even mystical interrelationships between the outside world and the creative world of the artist is to bypass what Roger Sessions calls the essence of music—"the gesture of the spirit."

Historical events can place certain musical periods for the layman. They are signposts for those who are more at home in what *happened* to man than in what he *did*. But they do not testify to the nature of music.

If, then, we do not embrace the two most popular approaches, the evolutionary and socio-historical, we still do not neglect to give them their marginal due. Even so, we are left with an important need: that of complete and exact systematization of the music between the years 1580 and 1790. It has not been attempted. Future scholars, it is to be hoped, will explore the field more thoroughly and prepare a detailed survey. Such work is beyond the power of one man and certainly beyond the scope of a booklet. But a systematized approach, slight as it may be at present, may help to clear up some of the puzzles and problems.

By not selling our souls to one or the other conventional approach, we remain unorthodox. No musical happening is being forced into a Procrustean bed of preconceived views. The thoughts expressed are perhaps only marginal. But hopefully we expect them to inspire where others only tread the didactic path. The intelligent reader will reach out further for investigation on his own and possibly refrain from waving any mental flag when looking at the history of music. Let him be suspicious of those who do so.

When, in 1941, Paul Henry Lang published his *Music in Western Civilization*, he could still complain about the dearth of available and easily accessible music material of the Baroque periods. Less than a quarter of a century later, much of this material has become available. An ever-increasing host of publications and numerous discoveries are broadening the base of performing groups dedicated to the performance of music from the early Renaissance to the late Rococo. They play on original instruments, from manuscripts, from up-to-date scholarly editions, and so on. In short, today's activities centering around this music are about as various as they were when it was first written. (Indeed, recordings and world-wide communications being what they are, performances are undoubtedly a manifold of what they must have been in the eighteenth century.)

This Baroque explosion proves that the music of our not so immediate past is a living matter, far too important to be left exclusively in the dry hands of scholars. Although scholars' unrelenting efforts have made possible current practices, the purely academic approach has given rise to a great number of misconceptions which, even today, cannot be dispelled entirely. Consider this example: Hugo Riemann, one of the more important modern musicologists, went to the original source and published it. For the student it became the only practical material. At the same time, his editions of Baroque and Rococo music are cumbersome and ornate in typically nineteenth-century fashion. Modern scholars quite rightly have attempted to counteract this romantic attitude. In doing so, however, they have made this music appear antiseptic and as devoid of life as the musty shelves on which for decades its original sources had rested unused and unsung. Unfortunately, their influence on the modern Baroque performers has been great; as a result many recent performances have left an unreal, lifeless impression upon the listener. Critics, always afraid to reveal their ignorance, approve of anything which smacks of scholarship. They extol such performances to high heaven, so that there still exists a general impression that the seventeenth century was devoted to the creation of mathematical formulas rather than living works of art. All over the world one can encounter a kind of performance that falsifies the picture to a similar extent, albeit in a different direction from that of romantic interpretation.

This IBM (International Baroque Monotony) approach has elicited two diametrically opposed reactions on the part of the general public: on the one hand, an immovable rejection of the Baroque and increasing ties to Romanticism with those who expect from music more than straight presentation; and, on the other hand, a new interest in Baroque music among those who, tired of nineteenth-century luxuriant chromaticism, the overheated climate of the operas of Wagner, and the outsized symphonies of Bruckner and Mahler, now can listen to music without becoming involved in it emotionally. Here, the contemporary listener finds what he expects from most modern music. He gets it in the cathartic Baroque performance without having to torture himself with the new and still unknown language of the dissonant and atonal counterpoint of the late twentieth-century masters. Thus, this decade is witness to two seemingly contradictory trends: a tremendous acceptance of the music of Mahler and Bruckner (only twenty years ago the bogies of American critics) and the Baroque explosion.

Fortunately, the increasing interest in Baroque music has also lured many nonspecialized performers to the fold of Baroque. With them, the valuable academic work of the scholar remains confined to research and the performance expands into a flesh and blood interpretation. With the aid of modern scholarship it also avoids the pitfall of romantic exaggeration.

Is it surprising that the vastness of music offered in a variety of performance styles leaves the lay listener baffled for all his love of it? At great historical distances, stylistic divergencies tend to merge into each other, and Monteverdi and Bach are easily thrown into the same pot. The untrained appreciation of the one who knows what he likes is merely an appreciation of himself, not of the arts. He is missing a chief esthetic prerequisite, the chance of comparison. He lacks the sense of roots and direction, of the cultural coherence. General interest in this music has grown so fast that valuable literature geared for the layman has had little chance to develop.

The modern listener is being bombarded by a number of styles and performances, each of which presents a separate and often quite argumentative point of view. An enlightening case in point is furnished by the "authentic" (historical) performance. More will have to be said about it in a later chapter, "The Baroque Performance." For the moment it suffices to consider only the audience reaction. No matter to what extent we create a technically and musically correct performance of the past—and we shall never be able to do so wholly, with modern musicians who lack their forebears' extended training and experience with the old instruments—its impact upon modern listeners will necessarily be quite different from what it was upon a Baroque public.

Let us examine, for example, the music of Johann Sebastian Bach, with which most readers are familiar. As a work of beauty, Bach's music possesses eternal verity. But as every man listens through the transport of the performance, he apperceives what is most akin to his inner self. Even the eternal truth of beauty, immutable though it is, changes its meaning in the process of apperception. While the laws of beauty remain constant as an abstraction of higher order, their materialization is relevant to the appreciator only in the context of the genesis of the work, its communicative value, and perhaps even its surface meaning. The grasp of the beauty, which is made by man for man, divine though it be, is placed within the boundaries that shape not only its creator, but also its recipient. When we speak of the timelessness of Bach's music, we really are saying that it conveys to us a meaning that goes beyond the limited horizon of our age as well as of that of its genesis. We divine that through it distant eras touch each other in a meeting of minds.

What Bach's music conveyed to the contemporaries of Mendelssohn it does not convey to us, and what it conveys to us it will not necessarily convey to our descendants. What we call the historical falsification of the romantic performance had emotional meaning in the nineteenth century for those who had just rediscovered Bach's music. They, in turn, might well have shuddered over our attempt at historical rectification in performance just as we shudder today over what we call the Victorian lack of taste.

Bach's music and appreciation of it are both of their own time and place. Had not this music been created as a thing of beauty, it could not have outlived the onslaught of so many diversified emotions on the part of listeners, as we can be certain that it will do so in the future.

Thus, no matter what qualities a specific performance of Bach may have, the work must have fallen differently upon the ears of the eighteenth-century Leipzig burgher than it does on those of the twentieth-century American businessman. Even if we could recreate fully the authenticity of a past performance, we could never do so in the mind of the modern public.

Are we then to reject the "authentic" performance? Not more so than any other type of a variety of performances. Obviously, we cannot control performances; frequently one type may be the only available sonic source of a specific work. But we can control our attitude toward, and understanding of, them.

Thurston Dart in *The Interpretation of Music* sums up the problem when speaking of the lute music of the older Gaultier: "No lutenist alive today has the technique and insight needed to do justice to this highly romantic music, and it cannot be played with its proper effect on any other instrument. We are judging the music by its appearance, therefore, not its sound. The ornaments which seem fussy on paper gave the greatest delight at the time they were written; the extravagant expressions of motion that are associated with the various moods meant a very great deal to the player of the 1630s. We have not the evidence for condemning the music; all that we can do is to try to discover what the seventeenth century thought about it, and apply what we learn to the interpretation of more accessible music written under its direct influence."

This book has been written with a similar relativistic point of view in mind. It falls into two parts. The first is a discussion of the nature of the music and its problems. This part should be read straight through.

The second part serves as a reference guide. The chapter "A Comparative Time Schedule" tries to place the reader within a frame of reference more familiar to him than the musical one. Musical events are put in historical parallel not only with historical but also artistic, cultural and technological happenings.

The chapter "The Musical Examples" is an analytical guide to the recorded works. Of course, frequent reference to them is also made in the general text.

The final chapter, "Composers' Biographies," enumerates the most important data of only those composers who are dealt with in the text.

In none of this do we aim at completeness. We are merely limiting ourselves to the instrumental music of the times under consideration. Nor is this limitation arbitrary. It is true that the greatest Baroque monuments are probably to be found in the field of opera and vocal church music. However, modern interest seems to center increasingly on the abstract; therefore, since the Baroque is the cradle of the purely instrumental style that today dominates not only our concert halls but modern music appreciation, this limitation seems justified.

In an active musical life of nearly forty years, the author has taken part in a variety of musical endeavors, which have led him through the most varied aspects of music, especially of the music under consideration here. Guiding various ensembles in the performance of Baroque works and producing a great number of phonograph recordings in cooperation with some leading modern interpreters, as well as serving as an editor and research student of Baroque sources, he has had ample opportunity to experience this music from both its academic and its practical aspects. There is something in the creative contact with a great number of performers that makes for a catholicity in taste and aids one in experiencing music as a living thing.

The author recalls with great joy the countless hours of arguments and deliberations with his colleagues. It is from such hours that a deeper musical conscience—and thus a greater sense of responsibility toward the performance—develops. For the serious performer all discussions culminate in one thought: Baroque music, like all other music, is played for its own sake, unburdened by extraneous messages. Yet it is not without inner meaning beyond the organization of its sounds.

Carl Philipp Emanuel Bach laid great stress upon the necessity of affect in the performer, which also arouses affect in the listener. It is this affect for which a good performance strives. Some of it, the author believes, has also gone into this booklet. Although knowledge and scholarship are imperative, only genuine musical material can come close to the essence of music. Similarly, the reader will find that reading about music is at best only a concomitant to the pleasure of listening, but never an end in itself.

This book then, in a sense, is the work of many musicians through many years. Their arguments are condensed in these thoughts, which, one hopes, may help the intelligent reader to find his way through that delightful maze of music that reaches from the Renaissance to our modern age.

2

THE ESSENCE OF THE BAROQUE

Sound, Style, and Form

When it was all over it had a name. Like Molière's Mr. Jourdain, who in his forties discovered that he had spoken prose all his life, the seventeenth-century composer maybe said to have discovered a hundred years after his death that he had been writing Baroque music.

The art historian Woelfflin applied the term originally to architecture, referring with it to what he called the "grand style." It was meant to describe such diversified architectures as those of Bernini and Borromini in Italy and of the brothers Asam and Fischer von Erlach in Southern Germany and the Palladianism of Wren and Inigo Jones in England. Woelfflin's definition was sufficiently vague and generalized to transfer the term later to other arts, such as literature, theater, and music. Benedetto Croce, taking a technical stand, insisted on its use as a description of the turgid and the craftsman's abuse of the materials in the arts. From these two trends, Woelfflin's classifying and Croce's pejorative nomenclature, there developed a variety of attitudes reflecting one view or the other.

In music, the term was highly confusing, because it was meant to cover a multitude of periods reaching from Viadana to Carl Philipp Emanuel Bach. In the mind of the public, it signified only the late Baroque, the music of J. S. Bach and Telemann. Yet, so strong had been the desire of the early seventeenth-century composers to break away from Renaissance music that enough stylistic common ground could be found in all music that ranged from 1580 to about 1750. Nor was what we can call the early Baroque revolution as unconscious on the part of the composers as one might at first assume. Their demand for "Nuove musiche" was sufficiently vociferous to center the attention of later generations upon its essentials.

It is due in large measure to the attempts at systematization and definition by Manfred Bukofzer that the term "Baroque music" as an established definition (without any further reference to the other arts sailing under a similar heading) came to be recognized universally.

Trends and shapes of modern Western European society were formed first in the early sixteenth century. The Reformation with its revolutionary peasant wars broadened the base of society. This initiated the development toward a mass society. Mercantilism and the evolution of civic communities in northern Italy and the towns of the Hanseatic League in Northern Germany gave rise to an economically strong stratum of burghers. Eventually, mercantilism advanced the cause of political absolutism which, hand in hand with the gaining Counter Reformation, created a new kind of court, full of lavishness and splendor. A rapprochement of church and state, which occasionally even led to church-state identity and an increasing consolidation of national states, did its part to differentiate this society from the medieval social organization. Its artistic demands became in many instances more conscious of a secular purpose.

The social position of the musician now assumed quite novel aspects. There existed two types of possible jobs. The composer could be employed by a sovereign court, such as that of the Roi Soleil in Versailles or any modest establishment in one of the countless small German duchies. He was paid well and mostly in kind; but for all practical purposes he was a serf. He had to wear livery and could not quit of his own free will. While such employment was perhaps more cumbersome, a greater prestige was attached to it than to other types of employment. For example, there were various musical, clerical, or civic institutions governed by the new burgher stratum in such communities as Hamburg and Venice. Here, the composer was engaged often "for life" after extensive competitive tests, but he was quite free to cancel his contract. Occasionally, such jobs could also be obtained in the modern manner through financial "kickbacks." Slowly, middle-class musical academies came into being. These private institutions were referred to as "Collegia Musica." They provided an opportunity for traveling on concert tours. The base was consistently broadened to the extent that the first truly "commercial" concerts took place in England toward the end of the Baroque.

A logical parallel to this development was the use of the musician as merchandise. Italy exported many musicians who, because of their exceptionally fine conservatory training, were in high demand. With this, a differentiating salary scale was applied to each type of musician. Trumpeters and kettledrum players claimed a higher salary because of the manifold possibilities of using them, such as, for example, as signal men in times of war or as *Stadtpfeifer* in times of peace.

Increasing commercialization gave rise to new music industries, such as the manufacture of instruments: stringed instruments in Italy by Amati and Stradivarius; organs in the North by Compenius Schnitger, and Silbermann; harpsichords in the Netherlands by Ruckers. The publication of printed musical material also became a lucrative business because of the lack of copyright protection. The frequently pirated editions with their inaccuracies and without printed date of publication are the bane of the modern scholar.

In these busy days of musical enterprise, the composers had to write for definite audiences and not for vague future immortality. They were bound in their work to the resources available to them in their respective places. But they had intimate contact with their public, which was interested and educated enough to accept the prevailing standards. No talk was heard then of writing down to the public, as it developed later in the days of broadest mass consumption. Music was written for specific occasions, which also included concerts in specific halls, whose size and acoustics often influenced the style of writing. (Today, in the days of high fidelity and authenticity vogues on the phonograph, it is hard to understand that record companies have but rarely explored the avenues of original acoustics. Certainly, an interesting picture could be obtained in recording music in halls that simulate acoustical conditions for which these pieces were written.)

Baroque music had three basic uses: first, *music for the theater*; that is, opera, music for the stage, and ballet, which frequently was merely an interpolation in a play; second, *chamber music* for the purposes of entertainment and edification; third, *church music,* an embellishment of the service.

Theater music was largely an effort of the courts. In the plays at the French court, the king and members of his household were active participants in the plays and pantomimes. Opera was performed only for those invited privately. Later efforts to make opera pay failed miserably.

Although chamber music flourished most in the musical academies, it was often used as background music to banquets (*Tafelmusik*) and pageants at the courts. But it was also employed for similar purposes by the clergy. Hence, musicians were drawn into both official and private church functions, and we find much affinity between the styles used for the two purposes, the *sonata da camera* and the *sonata da chiesa.*

Church music was for the most part vocal. But it, too, made use of the newly gained instrumental experiences.

All three types of music were influenced to a large extent by the dance element as it was employed traditionally and developed on the village green. The folk element was never quite absent. In the new, fast growing society it helped to broaden the basis of the audience and established the dance as an important stylistic substance.

The writing of music for special acoustics has had far-reaching consequences. The architectural layout of St. Mark's in Venice inspired the echo effects of the compositions of the younger Gabrieli. In further development they led to the significant terraced dynamics of the Baroque and also guided the ripieno and concertino contrast treatment in the concerti.

The great reverberation time in the large halls and churches also influenced the harmonic treatment; quick harmonic changes would have become unrecognizable, with one harmony echoing into the other. Certain composers calculated on the reverberation time and attempted to achieve special dual harmonic effects through it.

On the other hand, the small size and intimacy of many halls determined the volume of sound. Stringed instruments were on a lower level and played less stridently than when performed today even in so-called "authentic" performances. A really brilliant spiccato was absent, and so were extreme effects. Pizzicato was used but rarely, and only in order to achieve some special extra-musical impression. The dynamics centered around one level of medium volume. No gradual crescendi or decrescendi were known. The contrast as employed in the echoes and terraced dynamics (an immediate change-over from one sound level to another) were far less extreme than we are wont to play them in modern performance. Many of these contrasts were taken from the organ in direct imitation of the effects of its graduated registration.

Many "soft" instruments were employed. The virginal, with its one plane of sound, provided for performances on an uncomplicated level (record 1, side 1, band 9). The harpsichord (record 1, side 1, band 2) was not only a continuo instrument, but in its possible simultaneous employment of many voices lent itself excellently to the presentation of instrumental polyphony. Thus used, it presented a more intimate version of a larger instrumental body. The same may be said of the organ positive (record 1, side 1, band 5) and the guitar (record 1, side 1, band 4). At the same time, having the great, still almost medieval sense for his instrumental craft, the composer employed these instruments idiomatically as well. (See the lute, record 1, side 1, band 8.) The clavichord (record 1, side 1, band 3) was by no means, as is commonly assumed, merely an instrument for private practice in the manner of the modern silent keyboard. It was a practical performing instrument, whose interesting tremelo qualities were purposefully put to use (record 1, side 1, band 3). In addition, its abstract clarity served to outline two voices composed melodically against each other (record 1, side 1, band 10).

Occasionally, the specific sound quality of the harpsichord induced the composer to experiment with representational effects (record 1, side 1, band 6), and to indulge in imitative sounds (record 1, side 2, band 6).

At the same time a great deal of music was also written for outdoor use. Typical are the German *Stadtpfeifer* and *Turmmusiken*, which served specific purposes, such as indicating the hour, calling the community to religious service, announcing a special event, and so on. On account of the out-of-door use, their sound level was then considerably higher, though possibly less strident than that achieved in the modern parallels (record 1, side 1, band 1).

Two more factors contributed to the particular sound of the Baroque, pitch and temperament. It is not true, as is generally assumed, that the Baroque had no acute sense of pitch. Even such a marginal phenomenon as the ostensible decline of pitch at great volume in excessive reverberation length was taken into account by some composers, as witnessed by a number of contemporary theoretical writings. Yet, there existed no universal standard pitch, as there is today through our A = 440 vibrations per second. (Even the modern standard exists no longer; each of the great modern orchestras has a variance of pitch from 440 to 448.) But in the Baroque, depending on the specific decade and locality, pitch varied to a far greater extent. According to the research of Ellis, pitch varied as follows: 1619, Praetorius' "suitable" pitch of 424; 1648, Mersenne's spinet of 403; 1668, Tomkins' pitch of 474; 1688, St. James' Hamburg organ of 489; 1700, Rendsburg organ of 496; 1714, Freiberg organ of 420; 1739, Euler's clavichord of 392; 1751, Handel's pitch of 423; 1754, Silbermann organ at Dresden of 415. As this list shows, no definite trend can be established. But one thing is certain. Wherever ensembles played instruments which could be tuned on the spot (such as strings), they tuned them to the pitch of the fixed instrument (such as the organ). Often, for economic reasons, less tin was used for organ pipes, resulting in their shorter length and, thus, higher pitch. Whenever this pitch was too high for the other instruments to tune correctly according to it, either the music was transposed to a higher key (a simple matter for the skilled Baroque musician), or the organ pipes were exchanged for one another, in order to produce a lower pitch. Although musicians were pitch-conscious, it is quite evident that with the method described here of alleviating pitch variance, the intonation could not be as accurate (or rather what modern ears hear as accurate) as we are used to in today's performances.

This seeming inaccuracy was a concomitant of the natural tuning then in use. Only after tonality was established firmly, not only in practice, but also in numerous theoretical writings by Werckmeister, Rameau, Kuhnau, and others, did tempering, the division of the octave into twelve equal half-tones, as opposed to their pure or natural tuning based on the individual interval relationship, become a necessity. Even the early Silbermann organs were not tuned according to the new system. It was only at the time of J. S. Bach that equal temperament became definitely established. From this point excursions into more remote keys developed as a matter of course. No early Baroque composition was notated in, let us say, the key of F sharp major. Yet, in Bach's *Well-Tempered Clavier* this, like any of the possible twenty-four keys, is employed quite naturally.

In their own way, the Baroque musicians were as sensitive to the requirements of sound as are our modern ears, and they created an esthetic of their own, which was based on the factors then possible.

Numerous theoretical writings testify to the preoccupation with esthetics in the Baroque. These, ranging from Werckmeister's strict definition of music as a mathematical science to Heinichen's more journalistic approach, in which he makes taste (goût) and public approval the touchstone of music, prove that the Baroque was highly style-conscious.

Sébastien de Brossard writes: "Style means in general the particular manner of expressing ideas, of writing, or of doing some other thing. In music, it signifies the manner in which every individual composes, plays or teaches, and all this is very diversified according to the genius of the authors, the country and the nation; as well as according to the materials, the places, the times, the subjects, the expressions." This is already a very modern thought. More important, it stresses the basic belief in the fact that each piece of music creates different effects in both player and listener. De Brossard continues: "The style of gay and joyful music is very different from the style of grave and serious music." From there one arrives directly at Mattheson's description of musical material in terms of its effects. He speaks of "lovely pompous horns, proud bassoons, harsh cornets, modest flutes, heroic kettledrums, flattering lutes, grumbling bass fiddles."

The preoccupation with inner affects stems directly from the Baroque musicians' obsession with physical representation of the outside world. Beginning with Monteverdi, possibly because the Baroque revolution started with the invention of opera and its stress on the meaning of the word, composers attempted to depict the outside world—nature, animals, external changes (record 1, side 1, band 6, and side 2, band 6). This was done at first in strict sonic imitation. More sophisticated was the later pictorial representation of a larger program (record 2, side 2, band 2). Here, an acoustical frame served to express an imaginary state of the soul (joy, fear, hope).

From a combination of extraneous and internal descriptions, basic effects were gained. By eventual separation of the symbols from the effect purpose, the symbols became independent, and a whole set of tonal symbolisms developed to the point of mannerism. Well-known are the examples in Bach's music—at that time the whole system was already worked out completely and generally. Albert Schweitzer built his whole view of Bach on the examination of his tonal symbolism (descending steps for the interment, rapidly ascending scales for the joyfully heaven-rising angels, and so on). Certainly, the whole Baroque period is symbol-ridden. Much of its music is obviously manneristic, but while this is a vital feature, it is by no means the only one.

The affects are important, but in the last analysis they do not aim at identification in the Aristotelean sense. All together, they arrive at what characterizes this music most, at the pleasure principle. Lessing is the apt spokesman of the period when he says, "The final aim of arts is pleasure."

To reach this ultimate end, a variety of affects is conjured up. Thus, the entire period shows, at the same time, a certain unity of style expressed through the pleasure principle and a great deal of heterogeneity in its means of pursuing this goal.

The interplay of affects and symbolisms is an essential factor of giving shape to the form of the Baroque composition.

Initially, the Baroque had taken over external forms from the Renaissance. Certain formal shapes had been absorbed. Infused with a new style, they became a novel formal principle. Thus, once divorced from the vocal style, the concertato of the motets and the recitative of the madrigals developed into independent, new forms, which ceased to be external schemes. Growing out of an inner essence, they were the sum total of internal processes and not music draped around a scaffolding.

At first, the introduction of monodic elements by way of early opera had loosened the strict forms of the Renaissance. Very early, a trend to the merely rhapsodic was checked by unifying the diverse parts. To enhance the affects, strophic repetition of the ritornelli, which had been taken over from the opera, became a formal principle. The endless da capo established a need for new contrasts, which were achieved at first through performance. Through the entire Baroque, performers never played the same section in the same manner twice, but varied it by tempo divergences and new embellishments. Thus, variation in composition ensued, making it an essential formal element of the Baroque (record 1, side 2, band 4).

The Baroque variation, unlike its classical counterpart, strives for immediate contrast, not for the steady evolution of a theme. Out of the contrasted sections emerges ultimately the multisectional form, in which each section seems to have little to do with the next, the relationship being purely that of contrast; in the suite, the succession of dances follows the same principle.

A special variation species is the passacaglia or chaconne (record 1, side 1, band 2), in which an immovable ground maintains unity while the varied upper parts provide contrast. Here, the variation principle is demonstrated as a simultaneous event. In the variation form proper the same principle is exposed as a series of successive steps.

The middle period of the Baroque leads to an expansion of the smaller sections. The form becomes more established; the numerous small parts are replaced by fewer large segments, which eventually grow into separate movements. These movements look for definite formal articulation. The da capo, an outstanding means of such articulation, gives each movements its identity. The long stretches of repetitions, which because of the lack of imagination in the modern performer, may seem dull to our audiences, are, nevertheless, a vital form-building device.

Since every movement strives for one effect only, its style, be it the harmonic stress of simple tonality over a chordal scaffolding or a steady contrapuntal treatment, is the determining formal element.

Formal delineations are achieved as well through varied tempos. As Baroque music matures, these tempo contrasts take on additional importance, and this to such an extent that the arrangement of movements according to tempo develops into a set of formal principles. In its ultimate form, the *sonata da chiesa* consists of four movements: slow–fast–slow–fast. Earlier its articulation depended only on the stylistic essence of each movement, and the succession of contrasting tempos is not schematized as yet (record 1, side 2, band 1).

In general, the partition of the sonata into four basic segments remains significant. Telemann's *Solo Sonata,* with the common scheme slow–fast–slow–fast (record 1, side 2, band 3), and Heinichen's *Trio Sonata* (record 1, side 1, band 7), built according to the same tempo principle, are typical examples of the establishment of this formal tenet. Both sonatas prove that the same outer form, when invested with a variety of styles, can lead to quite different results. Thus, the immovable formal principle of the late Baroque (one must guard against attributing late characteristics to earlier periods) has not made music freeze in its track. The suite also follows generally the four-part principle, even when short dances are added to each larger segment. Only the concerto, possibly because of the more expanded form in the corner movements, relies on a three-part contrast: fast–slow–fast (record 2, side 1, band 2).

It would be a mistake to compare the establishment of strict form with the classical principle. The main difference lies in the preference of the Baroque for monothematic presentation. More important, the basic motif always remains in its nuclear shape. There never occurs any splitting off in the manner of the romantics. When a motif appears in a new harmonic guise, it does so unaltered in its shape. Even when worked through contrapuntally, it may possibly be presented in inverted, diminished, or enlarged shape, but it is never independently developed. And the same principle is adhered to even when another contrasting device, the juxtaposition of ripieno and concertino, is introduced. It is only with Vivaldi that several themes are presented in the same movement.

However, they appear in alternating sections, giving the movement a shape rather similar to the rondo. The themes may stand in different, though related keys, and the cadential return to the determining tonality of the movement is always followed through strictly.

In Vivaldi, the harmonic scheme of unalterable tonality becomes most apparent. The music moves from chord to chord in cadential relation, and even the concertante instrument rhapsodizes only in arpeggios of each functional harmony (record 2, side 1, band 2).

The great revolution of the Baroque, which eventually separates it completely from the Renaissance, lies in its use of and approach to harmony. It is a common mistake to consider all writing of the Renaissance exclusively polyphonic. There are a number of compositions that employ the note against note counterpoint, which subsequently results in a structure of chords. But the chordal writing of the Baroque differentiates itself from that of the Renaissance by the interrelation of the various chords to each other and to one basic key—in short, by the establishment of what can be called modern tonality. Out of the window goes the modal system, and the tonal system enters. Obviously, this does not happen overnight. But the evolution of the process is faster than one is prone to think.

It would be erroneous to believe that this kind of harmonic writing results only in homophonic compositions. The great novel achievement of the Baroque is its interweaving of harmonic (tonal) and contrapuntal (melodically interdependent) facets. With the stress of tonality, the extreme voices (melody and bass), which carry the harmonic structure by linear means, gain in importance over the inner voices. These, carrying out the counterpoint, require a special differentiation to be clearly recognizable, which leads to rhythmical refinement. Thus, the new tonality has its consequences not only in the harmonic field, but in the areas of dynamics (balance), rhythm (differentiation), and melody (stress of extreme voices) as well. All this laid the cornerstone of the language of music, as we have come to accept it far into the twentieth century.

The theoretical foundation of this new tonality, the functional harmony, is to be encountered in Rameau's famous *Traité de l'har-*

monie in which he wrote, ". . . melody is born of harmony." Rameau was not the first to recognize the new harmonic functionality, which he tried to underpin, although somewhat vaguely, with the overtone theory by Sauveur. But he was the first to codify the harmonic happenings of the Baroque up to his time; and he enlarged upon them by adding numerous imaginative thoughts of his own. For more than two centuries—up to Arnold Schönberg's *Harmonielehre*, which similarly codified the classic and romantic periods—his was the fundamental theoretical work on harmony. It demonstrates that the *harmonic* concept of the Baroque is its inherent unity.

3

THE BAROQUE PERFORMANCE

A Modern Dilemma

Once the essentials of Baroque music are arrived at, the musician is faced with the problem of performance. Here he encounters a serious obstacle, which lies in the inconclusiveness of the written or printed notes. With the classics the musical score presents a picture which, while open to a variety of interpretations, gives decided guidelines to tempo, dynamics, phrasing, and so on. Every note is to be played as written. Furthermore, a general standard of pitch and tuning exists.

This is not so in Baroque music. There are no agogic markings in the score. Ornamentation and execution of the continuo are left to the improvisational imagination of the performer. When this music was performed first, pitch and tuning depended on locality, that is to say, on the specific moment of execution. Originally, it was played under the guidance and with the participation of the composer. An aural—not a written—tradition was established. But the ear's recording is ephemeral. Without exact notation, much of what the ear hears is soon lost. The skilled Baroque performer was an expert in the art of improvisation; whereas the modern performer is limited.*

The execution of the continuo is most vexing. Early Baroque depended on one or two melodic instruments to develop a thematic substance over a ground played by a bass instrument (the viola da gamba or the violoncello). As the style veered toward the firm establishment of harmonic tonality, this sparsity of instrumentation proved insufficient to represent the harmonic essence. Thus, an additional instrument, such as the guitar, lute, organ, and most notably the harpsichord, because of their ability to play chords, proved most useful for this purpose. The bass line along with the melody identified the harmonic turns. Later, numbers were added to the bass notes, which in a sort of musical shorthand gave unequivocal indication of the harmonies required. Thus, the so-called "figured" bass developed.

It would be a mistake to consider the continuo instrument simply as an harmonic filler. Skilled performers executed the continuo by making use of melodic fragments as well. On the other hand, this sort of treatment was restricted, since no motival development in the classical manner was known. Therefore, proper and artful voice leading, resulting in the full expression of the harmonic intent, was the only basis for a stylistically correct continuo execution. Nor is the continuo merely added color. It must be heard—and heard clearly; yet, it takes a backseat to the melody and bass instruments. Its accurate sonic position within the music is highly

* In this connection it may be interesting to point out a special problem which arises from the use of the continuo on phonograph recordings, especially in regard to late Baroque and early Rococo. In this period the conductor used to conduct the orchestra from the harpsichord, occasionally filling in a chord on the harpsichord whenever fancy struck him or he had a hand free as well as when an harmonic filler was esthetically needed. Consequently, to play the harpsichord continuously with the orchestra, as happens on so many phonographic performances, is historically incorrect. Furthermore, it adds a percussive character to the piece, which in no way is esthetically justified. On the other hand, just an occasional sound of the harpsichord, which would be historically authentic, makes for a rather weird impression on a phonograph recording; whereas it might be completely acceptable in the hall. Indeed, it might be preferable to leave out the harpsichord completely in the phonograph performance in those instances where only an occasional harmonic filler is required.

important. In other words, the problem of balance arises, with respect not only to the relation of outer to inner voices, but also to the proportion of linear voices to chordal execution. Neither an excessively loud nor a simply coloristic harpsichord does justice to the purpose of the continuo.

With the question of balance, one encounters the problem of instrumentation. In earlier Baroque music there was little indication as to which instrument should play a melodic line. It could be a flute, an oboe, or a violin. There is never a precise identification of the continuo instrument. The decision as to whether it should be a lute, an organ, or a harpsichord depended on several factors. Historical research helps by inquiring into the time and place of the first performance. Such research can establish which type of instrument was in use at the specific locality at the given time. But this method may not always be satisfactory, for it merely anchors modern performance to a shibboleth. The composer may have used a flute because it was the only instrument at his disposal, but he might have preferred an oboe.

When a piece of Baroque music is indicative of a specific mood, it might be sensible to conclude from this mood which combination and what type of instruments would establish it best. The decision to use old-style instruments, such as the viola da gamba, must depend on the nature of the timbre they were meant to convey and whether this timbre is an integral part of the composition. It is then vital that modern performers using a different technique elicit the required timbre. The Baroque composer allots very specific moods to certain instruments: to the oboe the "pastoso"; to the flutes "les tendres plaintes." Thus, the choice of instrument depends on the indicated atmosphere of the piece. In more questionable cases, one must examine the polyphonic structure in order to arrive at a proper balance which, in turn, may determine the correct instrumentation.

With the choice of instruments there arises the question of dynamics, which is decided by the purpose of the piece. An outdoor composition calls for a higher sound level and less differentiated dynamics. In a work intended for a vast church, doubling of the instruments is required, and this in a manner that does not impinge upon correct balance. A string body for a piece by Rosenmüller, written for a small Hamburg congregation, may be correct with four first violins, while Lully at the French court may have needed sixteen.

A sufficient number of detailed descriptions of Baroque performances allows us to draw correct conclusions. For instance, the Monteverdi *Vespers* were performed in the following manner: orchestra, chorus, and soloists were distributed in separate groups throughout the building; each group had its continuo player who conducted it; the obbligato passages of the soloists sounded like improvisations and their individual passages reached the listener from different parts of the hall. Unfortunately, such an arrangement is seldom taken into account in modern performances; yet it is an essential part of the composition itself. The effect of sudden surprise is often an integral part of Baroque music.

If the entire orchestra is placed as a whole on the concert stage, the surprise element is lost. If the orchestra cannot be distributed throughout the concert hall, then the modern performer should construe an effect which simulates this.

The repeated echo effects point to the practice of dynamic contrasts; hence, they develop the terraced dynamics, with the concept of modern crescendo or decresendo wholly unknown. Since the echoes were contained within one hall, and not always a very large hall, their contrasts could not have been very marked. Consequently, performers must refrain from extreme dynamics.

The question of pitch has been decided for the modern performer through the standarization achieved in our time. It would serve no purpose, except an antiquarian interest, to try to simulate what one believes to be an older type of pitch or tuning, especially since, as we have shown before, no uniform pitch existed in the Baroque, and no perfect natural temperament could be achieved on modern instruments, which through their performers are geared to tempered practice.

The use of specific instruments determines the phrasing. This is one of the more complicated problems. Since Baroque scores contain no phrasing marks, we depend for information mostly on theoretical treatises and on our knowledge of what Baroque instruments could do. We know that the violins hardly ever used any legato but largely the clipped French détaché, and still sounded less strident than our modern instruments. The vibrato was unknown except for special effects, unless it was the natural property of the instrument itself, as in the clavichord. If we study some ancient fingering as it has come down to us on keyboard pieces, we notice that the contrapuntal articulation, which often is a problem of balance and phrasing was more important to the performer than a singing legato style. It was of uppermost importance that, whenever the theme recurred, it should be presented with practically the same type of phrasing.

Even without clamoring for the "authentic" performance, the modern performer must be aware of these facts if he is not to destroy the nature of the music he plays.

Proper phrasing can also be achieved through the examination of the ornamentation and its position within the composition; for, the ornament often subdivides the thematic structure. Both position and quality of the ornament give pointers to the manner of phrasing.

The Italians left ornamentation pretty much to the imagination of the performer. The French evolved a rather strict system of *agréments,* especially in keyboard music, which became fairly rigid and was the driving force in establishing a mannered style. The Germans took great pains with regard to accuracy; later on, they even noted down in detail the execution of the ornaments. Telemann repeatedly wrote out different ornaments. In his *Solo Sonata* (record 1, side 2, band 3), the first movement was written by Telemann first without the ornaments, and then with embellishments prescribed in every detail. On the record it is performed in both ways, illustrating the importance of correct ornamentation.

Embellishments constituted an essential stylistic element of the Baroque. Originally taken over from the vocal style of the Renaissance, where they had been both a means of virtuosity and an emotional expression, they took on a different meaning in the Baroque period. In the slow movements, where they were used most extensively, they served to make held notes sound longer in larger acoustics. Often their purpose was to loosen up the thematic stiffness. One must remember that in no instance was an ornament to be played in the same manner in parallel passages. Where ornaments did not belong to a fixed system, such as the French *agréments,* they gave the performer an almost unlimited choice of execution.

All embellishments combine melodic with rhythmic variance. The melody may start with the tone above the written note, lead into the written note, then feature the note below, return to the written note, and so on. This simple device has all sorts of rhythmic possibilities, so that even in those instances where the nature of ornament seems precisely indicated (through the generally agreed upon ornamental semantics), it is by no means unequivocally determined.

When the division between composer and performer increased toward the end of the Baroque period, more and more of the ornaments were written out. In a certain sense even Vivaldi's breaking of chords for the solo instrument in the concerti was a kind of harmonic ornamentation (record 2, side 1, band 2).

The entire principle of ornamentation was originally an incentive toward improvisation. This is demonstrated in the concerti where embellishments of the melodic line were requested of the solo instruments to a far higher degree than from the ripieno (tutti, orchestral) instruments. The improvisational aspect sometimes went so far that the composer merely indicated through several modulatory chords a bridge from one to the next movement over which the performer had to invent a melody. This, occasionally, led to the creation of an additional, complete, and new movement. Finally, the virtuoso cadenzas in the concerti developed from these and similar practices. In all da capo sections, which had to be varied in each repetition, similar great improvisational skill was required.

Yet, the performer must take care not to run wild. His freedom is set within the limitations not only of taste, but also of tradition. A very thorough study of the nature and purpose of each ornament, their differences being dependent upon mood, tempo, and melodic structure of the piece, is necessary for proper performance. Such study requires special knowledge, and herein lies the danger that Baroque performances may be relinquished to the "specialists." A conservatory training course in this field should be mandatory for every budding performer.

The nature and detail of the ornament depend in part on tempo. If it is fast, a less elaborate embellishment is indicated than when it is slow. The entire tempo question is baffling in itself. In general, no extremes were likely. Johann Gottfried Walther, in his *Musikalisches Lexikon* of 1732, gives some tempo definitions that prove that neither extremely fast nor extremely slow tempi were usual.

The tempo also determined the rhythmical pulse. It is a widespread misconception that Baroque performers played their music metronomically strict without the slightest tempo deviation. The Baroque was acquainted with the rubato, the imperceptible yielding in rhythm. Daniel Gottlob Türk, music director at the University of Halle in 1779, explained the tempo rubato as practiced then: "Commonly one understands by it a kind of diminution and prolongation of notes or a displacement of the same. Namely one takes away (steals) from one note some of its length and gives another that much more." The French refined this general and "free" principle to such an extent that the typical French rhythm schematized the rubato idea by making it a strict rule, in slow tempo, to shorten the briefer note by a half which was to be added to the longer note.

The problems of Baroque performance are so intricate that it is impossible for the layman (and frequently also for the expert) to decide which performance best meets the style. This raises once more the question of the so-called "authentic" performance which tries to recreate by scientific means the precise original conditions of an historic performance. We have shown before that this is neither wholly possible nor quite desirable, since it does not evoke the same reaction in the modern and the Baroque audience. On the other hand, it must not be condemned. Those who work at it seriously are, by no means, what Debussy called "musicologists poking their historical noses into matters that are not of their concern." If they fail, it is not their fault but the fault of the undertaking which is hampered by the irreducible change of time affecting everything that surrounds a performance: performer, instruments, acoustics, and listener. On the other hand, the efforts of musicologists create a healthy respect for historic scholarship in the modern performer, thus saving him from complete absurdities.

The performer who says, "I shall use the pianoforte instead of the harpsichord as continuo instrument, since I am also using the violin and not the rebec as melody instrument," is wrong. The piano introduces not only a dynamic imbalance but also a sound which has nothing to do with the Baroque style, whereas the violin still approximates the Baroque essence, especially when played in modified fashion.

Between the devil of complete elimination of the Baroque essence and the deep blue sea of a stilted and fake "authenticity," the modern performer must choose the happy medium. He will ask himself, "Which type of effect did this music strive for? How much of this effect can I recreate in the modern listener and by which musical means can I achieve it?" No great piece of sacred music will inspire a modern freethinker to the same kind of religious feeling which it generated in an eighteenth-century listener; but it can give the modern listener an inkling of the power that it may have had over those who in other times lived according to a quite different religious conviction.

The modern performer must use today's means of performance in expression, dynamics, and phrasing if he is to appeal at all to a modern audience. On the other hand, he cannot convert a three-hundred-year-old piece into a twentieth-century monstrosity without destroying its meaning. A judicious mixture of his modern musicianship, consisting of an up-to-date technique and contemporary taste together with knowledge of music history, should prepare him for a performance that is meaningful to the modern listener. Thus it will be modern and correct, for it takes into consideration the history of the composition. The performance does not spoil the music by raising it to an unreachable, hence unrealistic, plane through "authenticity," nor does it obliterate its nature by transferring it to a realm quite alien to its spirit.

The lay listener will do well to examine critically performances with exaggerated claims to authenticity as well as those which disregard the achievements of modern scholarship.

4

THE GREAT PERIODS OF THE BAROQUE

An Attempt at Historical Systematization

Any endeavor to squeeze achievements of the human spirit into a chronological system whose choice depends on convenient data must necessarily be arbitrary. Yet, to make such diverse figures as Monteverdi and Handel understood as the products of one era, a subdivision into sections, each of which has a community of characteristics that go beyond the unity of the total period, is imperative.

Several musicologists have attempted a logical arrangement. Suzanne Clercx distinguished between early (the last third of the sixteenth century), high (the entire seventeenth century) and late Baroque (the first half of the eighteenth century). More subtle is Bukofzer's division into early (1580–1630), middle (1630–1680), and late Baroque (1680–1730), which is, by and large, the one that we will follow.

The decisive connecting link between these periods is their overlapping; for many a seed laid in the earlier period comes to fruition at a later date. The time of development also varies from country to country. For instance, the middle Baroque starts later in the North than in Italy, and, when it was practically over in France, it reached a high bloom in England.

By deciding on the year 1580 as starting point, we find ourselves still in the Renaissance, and a delimitation of the new Baroque against the late Renaissance is essential. By determining the year 1750 as the end of the era (Bukofzer's date is 1730, but where does that put the late Bach and Handel?), we encroach upon the Rococo. However, an analysis of the Baroque's final notes and the transitory period into the Rococo throws an interesting light upon the significance of this period.

A. *The Early Period* (1580–1630)

The Reformation and the subsequent violent reaction against it had begun to give society a different face by the end of the sixteenth century. The emergence of regional churches broke the centralistic power of the Catholic Church. The papacy's secular domain was limited to the Papal States, which then were only a group among the great number of Italian states. Decentralization set in. Each town became a cultural community. The Church underwent imperceptible changes, with slight tendencies toward secularization. Its music turned into a means of recreation and was no longer an accessory of worship. This change brought to the fore the purely instrumental music. The spirit of humanism spread, especially in the North. At the same time the endless tug of war between Reformation and Counter Reformation, which lasted into the middle of the seventeenth century and of which the Thirty Years War was a climactic expression, furthered a return to medieval thought. This return became noticeable partly in the reaction of Catholicism and partly in the reaffirmation of the Protestant faith through a new kind of mysticism. The Commonwealth years in England, absolutism in France, with the king as the highest power of the state, the city-states in Italy, and the Hanseatic League secularized all cultural life, even though the secularization was mitigated by northern mystic pietism and the anticultural Cromwellian attitude in England. Music had come to be a secular power, which meant an independent cultural force.

Opinions differ as to the exact starting point of the new music, since no single event could have been decisive. The beginning was a process of change of attitude rather than an historical event. A few incidents highlight it.

Around 1580, in Florence, there came into being a group of amateurs, poets and musicians, who called themselves the Camerata. They met in the house of the socially influential Count Bardi and occupied themselves at the beginning with performances of madrigals. Amateurs, sometimes aided by professionals, performed for amateurs. They were the leading stratum of the growing merchant town. Gradually, under the prodding of Count Bardi, there developed a discussion on how to revive the classical Greek drama, a thought quite in keeping with the spirit of the Renaissance. Under the mistaken notion that all of Greek drama had been sung, Bardi tried to persuade the composers of the group to develop a style that would make it possible to express the fullest literal meaning of each word through singing.

Already some Renaissance madrigals had been accompanied by instruments which offered a harmonic digest of the music. Vicenzo Galilei, amateur lutenist and member of the Camerata, put these instrumental accompaniments to some use by occasionally inventing a type of madrigal which consisted of a single melodic line to the accompaniment of the lute. This type of madrigal differed from the traditional Renaissance madrigal only in the respect that it separated voice from instrument and condensed in the latter what would have been the sung parts in the traditional madrigal.

Galilei was probably the first to write a truly monodic melody with harmonic accompaniment. Not a revolutionary, he was little aware of having created something new. (When his teacher, the famous theoretician Zarlino, suggested that he tune the lute in twelve equal intervals, the tempered tuning that became a practical fact only more than a hundred years later, Galilei opposed this idea violently). But Bardi was quick to recognize the newness of the monodic treatment and its possible use for the resuscitation of the classical drama. He urged the composer Caccini, another member of the group, to try his hand at it. Caccini employed the method by setting some scenes of Bardi to music. This found much favor with the members of the Camerata. In 1600 the drama *Euridice* by the poet Rinuccini was set to music in this manner, some parts being written by Peri, others by Caccini. The style was crude. It was a succession of recitatives, but it was monody in extreme consequences; and the vocal line was already expressive of the individual words. (Somewhat earlier, in 1597, Rinuccini had written an opera libretto *Dafne,* which was set to music by Peri; but apparently it was never performed and the score has been lost.) Thus, there was born around the turn of the century the species "opera," an entirely new form of art.

More important, a consequential style, which was to be a determining factor in all fields of music for the coming years had entered upon the scene.

Groups similar to the Camerata, led by merchant princes and other secular rulers, also existed in other northern Italian towns. These groups were representative of the rising stratum of traders and burghers, and their cultural aspirations were decisive for all of Italian society. Monteverdi, then in Mantua at the ducal court, took up the Camerata's challenge. When he wrote his first opera, *La Favola d'Orfeo,* in 1607, he was already able to refine on the style. Already in 1605 he had written an essay, "Seconda pratica, ovvero perfettioni della moderna musica," in which he stressed the supremacy of the word over the music. His view was opposed to that of the traditionalists, whose music he called the "prima pratica," while his, as the one coming later, was named by him "seconda pratica" or "modern music." He was as conscious of creating something revolutionary as another great operatic composer, Richard Wagner, whose violent dispute with Hanslick reminds one of the disagreements between Monteverdi and Artusi, the exponent of the "prima pratica."

The recitative was sung with a great deal of pathos and emotion in order to create strong affects in the audience. This, in keeping with the intention of classical revival, was the Camerata's main purpose. In order to achieve the necessary affect the composer had to start, in the words of Caccini, "with a consideration of word and rhythm and then tone, and not the other way around." It is clear that such ideas had to reject any contrapuntal treatment which would have rendered the words unclear. Thus, Galilei attacked in his theoretical writings any manner of contrapuntal device. He who had used for his first monodic experiments pure poetry, an expressive passage from Dante's *Divina Commedia,* Ugolino's plaint, and the lamentation of Jeremiah from the Old Testament, furnished Caccini with enough stylistic ideas to start him on his way toward opera. And Caccini himself said that in his few years of association with Bardi and his ideas he had learned more about music than in "thirty years of contrapuntal study."

Monteverdi caught on to the new trend and his great genius began to elaborate upon it. The effect of the recitative was underlined by special effects in the instrumental accompaniment. Suddenly tremoli in the strings were introduced, and the concitato ("agitated") style was created in order to enhance dramatic effects. In *Il Combattimento di Tancredi e Clorinda,* Monteverdi dramatized each detail with pictorial means and developed a whole set of symbolic mannerisms.

These newly gained instrumental effects soon made themselves independent from the musical context, and in 1617 the composer Biagio Marini published his *Affetti musicali* for various instruments which employed all sorts of novel instrumental tricks. The idea of color took hold; Giovanni Gabrieli used it extensively, both instrumentally and vocally, as well as through his differentiated placement of various groups throughout the church. From this placement evolved a further coloristic idea, that of juxtaposition of tutti and solo passages, out of which the concerto style eventually developed.

The instrumental style which now grew independent from vocal music had its basis in the various purely instrumental interludes of the madrigals and in the eventual interpolation of *balletti* in the scenes of the dramatic plays. From a mere accompaniment it broadened out into a style of its own. This, too, had its forerunners in the Renaissance: for example, the instrumental dance music either for instrumental groups, by Claude Gervaise, or for the lute alone, by Gaultier and others. But it was now something new because of its tendency to introduce a leading upper melodic voice, which eventually was to determine the entire style of the composition. Thus, a new unity between form and technical means was created. Slowly, the harmonic modes tended to disappear and to give way to a limited tonal treatment.

It is quite unimportant whether we can place the beginning of the Baroque music with the publication of Caccini's monodic songs to lute accompaniment in his *Nuove musiche* (the title even is significant), or with the coloristic experiments of Monteverdi and Gabrieli. One thing is certain, around 1600 begins a development which winds up in a monodic recitativo style that is strictly opposed to extended contrapuntal treatment. It makes use of experimental instrumental effects. It is still partly modal, but its modality aims at an interrelationship between chords and underlies a new harmonic concept which might be called early tonality. An interesting example of this style is found in Merulo's *Toccata* (record 1, side 2, band 2), where the substance appears at times in the upper register and at others in the lower without any geniune counterpoint developing against it. The modality is obvious, at the same time the extensive use of the upper leading tone creates an harmonic ambiance which hints at future things to come.

The step from vocal to independent instrumental music took place in Italy earlier than anywhere else. In Germany, it was readily accepted by those communities in which municipal bands and *Stadtpfeifer* had a reason for being by dint of their communal functions. Under the influence of the new instrumental style they performed these functions in an artful form. Eventually, the *Turmmusik* was no longer a series of simple signals but developed into well-constructed suites under the influence of dance music, as shown in Pezel's compositions (record 1, side 1, band 1). The last country to follow Italy's example was France, where one of the early Italian practices, that of transcribing vocal canzoni for a group of instruments, gave the initial impetus.

With the instrumental canzoni there began a stylistic trend toward homophonic music. Although at first the unity of this style seemed threatened by the merely dramatic—hence, rhapsodic expression of the recitativo style—there appeared a serious effort to save it from this fate. This was achieved through a technique of variation on the original theme. The first hesitant attempts to vary the primary dramatic statement were made as early as in the above mentioned *Toccata* by Merulo (record 1, side2, band 2). The preponderant melody, as first introduced by Caccini and Galilei, developed in semivaried form over a static ground in tonal harmonic treatment. This was the base from which the sonata developed.

The sonata emerged first as instrumental canzone. Since it was a transcription of a vocal piece, it strove for idiomatic instrumental expression. In the early ecstasy of their newly found freedom, composers experimented wildly with instrumental effects. The sonatas of Possenti and Giovanni Valentini are full of tremoli, harmonics, pizzicati, and col legno bowings. Farina goes so far as to imitate animal sounds on the violin, an idea later taken over by other instruments as well (record 1, side 1, band 6).

Soon the sonata ceased to be a transcribed piece and became a composition in itself. The term originally signified a piece played by instruments. As the tonal concept developed, there was added to the upper voice and bass the harmonic detail by way of the continuo instrument, such as the harpsichord, organ, lute, or guitar. Thus, a solo sonata was played by three musicians: the melody, bass, and continuo player. In the trio sonata a second melody voice was added and we have four players, two for melody, and two for continuo.

With the addition of a second voice, a gradual return to contrapuntal treatment ensued. Now the bass took on a more characteristic aspect. It, too, changed into a melodic line as the concept of tonality developed. More than a simple succession of harmonic clusters was expected from the linear instruments, which can move with greatest melodic ease and therefore seem turgid and dull if they proceed in heavily pounded notes only. The trio sonata thus evolved from the instrumental canzone in which a kind of fugato style had been immanent in the form of the early type of the fugue, the ricercare. Historically, it started out as a canzone with bass and continuo added. The earliest specimen was a work by Salomone Rossi around 1607. The two treble instruments remained high up, while the continuo bridged the gap between them and the low bass. A similar contrast of extreme regions is found in the solo sonata of which Biagio Marini offered one of the first interesting examples in 1626.

From the early primitive species emanated two distinct types, the chamber sonata, or *sonata da camera,* and the church sonata, or *sonata da chiesa,* which, although they flourished in the middle Baroque to a large extent, are best discussed at this, their genetic, point.

The *sonata da camera* was initially the instrumental overture to early operas. As a preparation for the general mood of a larger concept, it consisted chiefly of a succession of little dance tunes, all in one and the same key. Gradually there was added a slow introduction to provide a preparatory feeling. This scheme was taken over from the Italians by the Germans, who developed it further. Rosenmüller modeled his sonatas after the Venetian theater *sinfonie* (overtures) of Cavalli and by 1667 had established a formal norm consisting of the following movements: sinfonia–allemande–corrente–intrada–ballo–sarabande. As other influences made themselves felt, the form expanded. Kusser enlarged the first movement in the manner of Lully's French overture and employed the typical French rhythm. He also turned the first movement into a tripartite structure after the French scheme: slow–fast–slow.

The *sonata da chiesa* was originally an instrumental interlude between vocal pieces in the church service. The term appeared first with Vitali around 1667, but the species existed before then, when it was a simple condensation of several short sections of instrumental canzoni into three or four movements. Since the Catholic Baroque Church was spiritually serene, the *sonata da chiesa* also employed occasionally gay, folkloric tunes. A strong contrapuntal fabric differentiated it from the *sonata da camera.*

There was no strict formal scheme at first (see Vitali, record 1, side 2, band 1), but eventually it evolved to a norm of slow–fast–slow–fast, with the last movement usually a dance tune.

Today, it is logical to use the organ as a continuo instrument for the *sonata da chiesa* and the harpsichord for the *sonata da camera;* but this is by no means obligatory, since both instruments were used in church and in private concerts.

Originally, the distinctions between the two species were not very strongly felt and were eventually completely lost in Corelli. His *sonate da camera* retained contrapuntal texture, whereas the last movements of his *sonate da chiesa* were often treated homophonically. In Purcell and Kuhnau the distinctions were even less evident.

The ultimate development of the sonata led to the large suite. Non-dance movements were interpolated between the dance sections of the *sonata da camera,* and a larger unity between the individual sections was established. The original suite, initially simply an illogical succession of dance pieces, developed into a piece of almost symphonic proportions while the sonata lost its shape gradually.

An interesting example of later years (1692–1726) are the *Sonates et Suites de Symphonies* by Couperin, which fall into two parts. The first was originally an early *sonata da chiesa* (record 2, side 1, band 3); whereas the second, a series of dances, was tacked on to it later (record 2, side 2, band 1). So skillfully was this done by the great French master that actually a huge structure was erected, in which the individual parts were linked very closely. With a typical French predilection for the dance and theater, Couperin gave the work a title referring vaguely to the nature of the dances and thus introduced, albeit seemingly, a programmatic element.

For the execution of the sonatas and suites the instruments with the proper range available at the moment were used. In seventeenth-century Italy we find a preference for strings, which may have something to do with the high virtuosity of most Italian musicians. According to Praetorius' *Syntagma musicum*, the most valuable theoretical work of the seventeenth century, instruments of similar range and movability were interchangeable in instrumentation. But wherever the color concept gained an upper hand, such as with Monteverdi and Gabrieli, the choice of instruments was unequivocal. It became even more so when composers began to write idiomatically. Vivaldi made a strong distinction between solo and tutti propensities of the instruments.

Often, composers took over the style from one instrument and transferred it to another of similar technical characteristics. The lute *Prelude* by Bach and the keyboard *Prelude* by d'Anglebert played on the virginal (record 1, side 1, bands 8 and 9) stem from one and the same musical concept and adapt themselves to the idioms of two different instruments. Doubling of voices was not usual, especially in the recitativo style. Only much later did there develop the orchestral recitative in unison.

The initial step from vocal to instrumental music had been taken by providing the madrigal with an instrumental bass. Madrigal composers had already written vocal variations over an "ostinato" bass prior to this and thus had laid the primary groundwork for the ciaconna. In this treatment composers had first become aware of the carrying powers of the bass as an harmonic force. It has never been quite established at which point the thorough (figured) bass* came into use. Probably it was around 1597 with Caccini and Peri. We definitely find it in Viadana's *Concerti Ecclesiastici* in 1602. Its first theoretical mention is made in 1607 in Agazzari's treatise *Del sonare sopra il basso*. But it gained its universal foothold only after Germany's first opposition to it was overcome by Scheidt in 1617. It certainly helped greatly in the development of the trio sonata. It was such a definite, indispensible stylistic feature of the Baroque that as late as the middle of the eighteenth century Philipp Emanuel Bach still could write: "No piece can be performed well without the accompaniment of the clavier (continuo) instrument.' Riemann calls it "the touchstone of the Baroque.'

Indeed, the thorough bass determined the style. It allowed the quickest melodic development over the ground, implied a definite harmonic structure, and even helped to establish instrumental balance. The Baroque did not develop because of it; rather, continuo practice developed because of the Baroque. Bukofzer summed up its significance in a few words: "The invention of the continuo was a symptom rather than a cause. With it all aspects of melody, harmony, and counterpoint appeared in a fundamentally changed perspective. For the first time there emerged in music history an harmonic polarity between bass and soprano, between harmonic support and a new type of melody dependent on such support. This polarity is the essence of the monodic style. With the new function of accompaniment relegated to the bass, the melody gained freedom and agility." Thus it helped to develop, and, ultimately, to establish firmly, the novel functional harmonic relationships.

With the new harmonic concept the metric principle also underwent changes. The meter of the later Renaissance dances, either double or triple time, had been accepted at once by the early Baroque. When the tonal concepts of functional harmony used cadential endings as a means to establish form, a combination of time and harmonic elements (both being interdependent) created a new concept and practice of the metrical elements.

* The bass here is the carrier of the harmonic fundamental with chords to be erected over it by a continuo instrument indicated by numbers in a kind of musical shorthand.

In Gabrieli the alternation of double and triple time was structural. From him it was transferred to Germany by way of Schütz, Gabrieli's most important pupil. Schütz also brought the true recitativo style to Germany and, with it, all the coloristic effects and tonal symbolisms that were to turn out so important in Bach.

When the melodic lines loosened up, as in Viadana's *Concerti ecclesiastici*, rhythms grew more differentiated. When these reached Germany, they influenced, at first, Schein, who in his *Geistliche Konzerte* achieved a varied meter. This love for variety induced him to accompany his vocal monodies on the instruments in a manner far more diversified than that of the Italians. In general we find in the Germans much earlier and, to a far greater extent, an inclination toward dense instrumental texture. The ricercare, taken over from vocal compositions, occupied an important place in German music, most notably in that of the greatest German keyboard master of his time, Froberger (record 1, side 1, band 5).

Great rhythmic variety was also displayed in the organ compositions of Scheidt, who invented the most unbelievably fascinating polyphonic patterns against a cantus firmus. The introduction of this style is significant of the northern countries.

With the rise of Protestantism, the church chorale became the mainstay of the church service. In the great argument between the Lutheran orthodoxy and Pietism and Calvinism, which was to extend into Bach's time, the chorale gained added importance. For the Pietists and Calvinists it was the expression of the individual's mystic union with God; for the Lutherans it became the scaffold upon which the artful music of the Church was to be built. Thus all through the Baroque period from Scheidt to Bach, the organ prelude was an important religious expression of the North. Taking a popular chorale melody as an underlying voice, or cantus firmus, the composer varied over and with it other voices. Between each such varied verse of the chorale he interpolated interludes which took their motival clue from the preceding variation and led into the next one (record 1, side 2, band 5). An important variation form was invented here, which should prove even more significant for the future than the passacaglia and variation sets, because it contained the first indication of a separate split-off motival treatment, a basic feature of later classicism.

We find the practice of the chorale prelude particularly strong in the Netherlands, where Sweelinck was the great master of organ music. Despite the influence of the Venetian school, he evolved his own style in which the development of the fugue was most remarkable. He was the first to vary not only the subject but also the countersubject.

From there the influence spread to England, which always showed a great predilection for the variation form for which the keyboard instruments furnished the most idiomatic means. (record 1, side 2, band 4). Orlando Gibbons, to mention the foremost master of the early period, and the virginalists, unlike the composers in other countries, did not take their cue from their vocal music but developed a keyboard style under the influence of the instrumental products of foreign nations. This trait of English music remained with it and reached its apex in Handel.

Along with the instrumental achievements, the mixed ensemble (consort) music of voices and instruments was remarkable. It was brought into Germany by groups of English comedians and violists who influenced the form of the German dance suite, which at the same time had also come under the spell of the suite form of the French lutenists and clavecinists. Consequently, the German suite is ultimately the result of multinational influences, that is, the Italian by way of Rosenmüller, the French and the English. With the latter two influences the virtuosi gained new impetus. They invented completely new effects, such as those of Biber, who tuned his violin differently (*scordatura*), in order to achieve novel expressions by new technical means.

This takes us far into the middle period of the Baroque.

B. *The Middle Period* (1630–1680)

What in the earlier years had been trends now became an established style. The recitativo style was smoothed out and developed into a singing aria (bel canto) style. The forms expanded from small sections into intricate edifices. Counterpoint again gained a foothold. The modes were reduced to two: major and minor. Basic tonality was the exclusive harmonic concept. Chromaticism amounted to little. The one important chromatic innovation was the Neapolitan sixth, the turning downward of an upward leading tone, which had been taken over from the Phrygian mode, but was put to quite novel and highly important use in the new tonality.

Two distinct styles developed, the French and the Italian. The French, using the woodwinds more profusely and employing a great deal of ornamentation, preferred suites and overtures. The Italians excelled in sonatas, sinfonie, and concerti. They used fewer embellishments, except in the adagio movements. In general, their style was more energetic and affective. The writers of the period distinguished quite well between the two styles. Raguenet wrote in 1713: "the French flatter and tickle the ears. . . . The Italians are interested in everything which sounds unusual, even rough. . . . They understand the passionate emotions and express them therefore better in their works. . . . Next to the instruments which are common to both French and Italians, we French also possess the oboe, which in its simultaneously soft and penetrating tone has a tremendous advantage over the violins in all fast and vivacious movements, and secondly the flute, which, as it is being taught successfully by many of our great artists, knows how to lament in mournful movements movingly and to sigh enamouredly in the tenderly moving sections." There crept in an awareness of the different affective possibilities of each instrument, which fixed instrumentation more definitely than in earlier days.

But despite the awareness of the two styles, most composers continued to write alternatingly in both. Yet, as society moved away from the supranational state of the Middle Ages and created a variety of separate national states, each with its own religion, music loses also its general so-called "European" character, and any investigation of it must be undertaken along national lines.

This national development was noted most strongly in Germany, where, after the terrible devastation of the Thirty Years' War, Protestantism had gained a firm foothold. The consequence of this was a strong decentralization of power and, with it, the relegation of culture to various individual communities, be they the powerful towns of the Hanseatic League or the numerous small duchies. Along with this decentralization went a certain provincial outlook, which Germany has not lost even in our day. It was underlined by the Protestant attitude, which stressed the democratic participation of the community in the religious service. Thus, the Protestant chorale developed as a unique feature of German music. The chorale was the main material out of which the great organ works of Tunder and Buxtehude were fashioned. Many composers from Praetorius onward occupied themselves with the problem of the harmonization of chorales. Out of this preoccupation grew the tremendous harmonic development that finally made Germany the country of the most involved chromaticism, while at the same time the complex variation technique of the chorale prelude prepared the ground for the later motival development in the classics.

Strict Protestantism turned its back upon the frills of the French and even upon the Italian style. Calvinism was so adamant in this that music came to a virtual standstill in the countries where it had reigned supreme. But as the Counter Reformation became more effective, especially in Austria and Bavaria, and such new national states as Brandenburg—Prussia began to gain greater importance and, with it, a more international outlook, foreign influences made themselves felt.

Froberger, the outstanding pupil of Frescobaldi, Italy's great keyboard master, assimilated not only the influences of his teacher, but also absorbed those of the clavecinists and the virginalists. In contrast to the northern German organ masters, he developed a loosened-up keyboard style that became a model for the composers of South Germany and Austria.

The development of the dance suite in Germany also took place under the influence of foreign stylistic elements. Much dance music had been played in Germany during the late Renaissance, possibly because of the strong agricultural nature of the German states in which the peasants played an important economic role. Peuerl's *Bäurische Tanz,* the *Quodlibets* of Melchior Franck, and the use of dances in the signal music of the *Turmmusiken,* and the *Stadtpfeifer* music stressed the dance element.

But in the Renaissance there had always been a marked difference between the dances of the peasants, which were simple and employed a straight, constant rhythm, and those of higher society which used a number of rhythmical types. Both had only one thing in common: each dance consisted of two contrasting sections, one in double meter and the other in triple meter. The typical double-meter dance had been the paduana, better known as the pavane, and the triple-meter dance was the galliard, saltarello, and courante. Out of these archetypes there developed a number of dances. Under various foreign influences the German dance suite, already existent in limited fashion with Rosenmüller, was carried to a new height by Hammerschmidt. He expanded the form by adding symphonic movements, such as intradas and overtures, and took over from the French the da capo arrangements of double bourrées, and other forms.

Around 1630, there began a new significant development in Italy, that of the bel canto style. In a reaction against the amateurs' demand for supremacy of the word over the music, composers attempted to give the singers parts that corresponded to the demands of the musical thematic substance rather than to those of the text. The new style of the wide, thematic melody spread from opera to instrumental music. The monodic style rose to supreme height. The strong emphasis on melody required only a simple harmonic scaffolding, for which the basic functional tonality provided an excellent means. Italian harmonic treatment remained rudimentary until (and including) Vivaldi.

Music had its center in the capital of France as the natural result of gaining absolute power for the court at Versailles. This, perhaps, gave it this long-lasting, amazing stylistic unity. But Baroque music took hold only slowly, and then in the special guise of the French variant. Largely, it was an expedient of the state. As such, it concentrated on the ballet, which became the apotheosis of the king under Louis XIV. The ballet de cour was performed by the "Vingt-Quatre Violons du Roi," which already under Louis XIII had reached the highest reputation. At that time this was the only large-scale orchestra in Europe. Since the great number of instruments was quite capable of filling out the necessary harmonies, the addition of a continuo instrument proved unnecessary until about 1650. This not only effected a different style than that of the thorough bass, but also freed the continuo instruments for their own independent uses.

In consequence, the organists created a style which took on a great many ornamental effects from the clavecinists and contributed some of its own by making extensive use of the coloristic possibilities of the organ.

The lute reached a high degree of virtuosity. Under Louis XIV it was replaced by the guitar, which excelled above all in dance suites, a random succession of dance pieces (record 1, side 1, band 4).

The clavecin, in a variety of applications ranging from the virginal to harpsichords in numerous shapes, took its cue from the lute and its virtuoso embellishments (record 1, side 1, band 9). A whole school of clavecinists, after transcribing operatic pieces for the keyboard, developed a style of its own, whose agréments created a set of mannerisms characteristic of the French style in general. Many pieces were a programmatic imitation of animal noises and similar jokes. From Chambonnières the development reached into Germany by way of Froberger, and such composers as Kerll found themselves in direct imitation of the French (record 1, side 1, band 6). The dance suite became a favorite composition for the harpsichord. But it was only Couperin who, under the influence of Lully, developed the suite into a genre of its own through additions of sections from the trio sonatas.

There are some authorities, such as Bukofzer, who hold that France experienced true Baroque music only in Lully. Couperin, the clavecinists, and Rameau are considered Rococo composers. This is perhaps too strict a view, since it minimizes Lully's influence upon the whole development of French music.

Lully was an Italian, who, at an early age, had come to France, where he held an important post at court throughout his life. He brought several Italian influences to France. These he developed single-handedly, thus creating new genres. Of them, the overture is the most important. It is divided into three sections: the first begins with dotted rhythms, later to become the main characteristic of the French style; it goes over into a second, fugal part, which is an imitation of the Italian instrumental canzone; the third section is a da capo of the first part. Lully also developed the instrumental chaconne, whose form he changed into a strict rondo. While his main achievements lie in the field of opera, the instrumental advances, all used at first in his operas, were to be of great consequence, not only in subsequent French music but also in Vivaldi, Handel, and Bach. Thus, the Italian point of departure had been decisive for France as well.

In Spain this point of departure was even more influential. Instrumental music was limited to an extensive practice of the guitar and lute and, in the latest Baroque period, to some chamber combinations, as in the works of Soler. But, except for the fact that archaic features lasted longer in Spanish music than in any other, Spanish composers were wholly dependent upon Italy.

The Italian influence made itself felt also in English music, which in pre-Cromwell days reached its climax in the consort music, instrumentally a combination of violas and violins. Jenkins, under some influence of the Italian trio sonata, developed the fancies, polyphonic instrumental pieces, in a manner that gave them a more graceful and melodically pleasing form. The mainstays of instrumental music were the masques, to which it provided an accompaniment. Harpsichord music consisted originally of simple dances, but reached a fantastic height in the virginalists who developed a keyboard style in which dance and variation forms played a decisive role.

The Cromwell interlude had a curious effect upon English music, but did not, as was assumed for a long time, destroy it. It retarded the evolution of that music; thus, we see in Purcell, the great genius of the Restoration period, the paramount influence of the Italian trio sonata, which in other countries had become manifest at a much earlier date. But the earlier, typically English penchant for variation over a constant ground also remained strong in Purcell (record 1, side 1, band 2). With him English Baroque music reached its apex. The next great English period was the work of a foreigner, the German musician Handel.

C. *The Late Period* (1680–1750)

With the last period we enter an era which contains everything popularly associated with Baroque music in general. The religious arguments within the two great churches have subsided and the era of full secular thinking is dawning. This is the age of both, the intellectual romanticism of Rousseau and the clear rationalistic thought of Voltaire. Little wonder then that also in music the duality of utmost clarity and spiritual involvement reigned supreme. Here, then, we encounter fullest tonality, with exacting treatment of the dissonance and increasing chromaticism. The large forms reached their ultimate expanded shape. Orchestra music gained preponderance over chamber music as the concerto slowly pushed aside the sonata. Counterpoint established itself strongly within the confines of tonality; a piece not written in the general polyphonic style was rare. (Vivaldi and Domenico Scarlatti are perhaps the composers with the least polyphonic leanings in this period.) The strongly polyphonic style of Bach is an important landmark.

The firm establishment of tonality had a number of far-reaching consequences. Counterpoint developed not only along melodic, but also along harmonic, lines. A new, rich kind of polyphony absorbed within its framework all those notes that heretofore had been dissonant tabus. Tonality determined the structure upon which large forms were built with a central key providing the unifying center. Alternation between homophony and polyphony provided new structural contrasts. In short, a whole new language of music that had been fermenting slowly since the days of the Renaissance came into full bloom.

Until then, each section of a composition had one theme, one mood, and one effect. Then, the orchestral concerto started to differentiate thematically between the tutti and solo material; the secondary theme was introduced for the first time, and the monolithic structure gradually weakened, although even then the secondary theme was merely a contrasting—not a derived—device. Only in the fugue did the secondary theme incorporate motifs that stem from the primary statement. With this there opened up the spiritual world of classicism.

In spite of all the stylistic community of the late Baroque, one must still differentiate between three national styles. The Italian style relied to a large extent on the resources of the new tonality. It excelled in the form of the concerto and sonata (sinfonia) to such an extent that, for the first time, instrumental treatment influenced vocal treatment, which was quite a reversal from earlier trends.

The French style stressed color and program. With it went the development of fixed ornamentation and a preference for the suite, that is, dance music.

In the German style we find a perfect unification of harmonic and contrapuntal material. This style followed its own inclination. But generally the unification of the three styles, the French, Italian, and German resulted in the so-called "style galant" by the middle of the eighteenth century.

Even at this time when exact instrumentation was prescribed, it was by no means always determined how many instruments would play an orchestral voice. Muffat conceded in 1701 that, in case of lack of a larger body, his concerti could be performed by two solo violins, a small bass, and harpsichord. He even permitted the omission of the inner voices if no violas were available. Torelli declared in 1708 that violas and basses could not only be doubled but also be enriched by theorboes and harps. The color concept was not developed to a degree of extreme exactitude.

In general, one notices a steady enlargement of the orchestral body. In 1730, J. S. Bach asked of the authorities an orchestra with twenty to twenty-four men. These were to be allotted the following instruments: two to three first violins; two to three second violins; two first and two second violas; two celli; one bass; two to three oboes; one to two bassoons; three trumpets; one group of timpani; and two flutes. At about the same time the Court Orchestra in Dresden under Hasse had twenty-five string players—eight first violins, seven second violins, four violas, three celli, three basses—and a great number of windplayers. The steady trend toward orchestral enlargement was checked only by economic necessity.

At that time the orchestra was an important instrument in Italy. Alessandro Scarlatti composed the overtures to his operas in the grand manner. They provided the direct bridge to the concerti grossi of Corelli. In 1685 Bononcini wrote independent sinfonie also for a larger orchestral body. In 1692 Torelli embarked upon the composition of several sinfonie and concerti. At first, the latter are simply orchestra concerti without solo parts. But gradually he split off a solo instrument from the tutti by writing solo interludes between the sections. He was the first to differentiate clearly between concertino and ripieno as a formal principle. He also established what came to be the classical concerto form: the three-movement work, consisting of allegro–adagio–allegro.

The formal idea of the concerto consisted of a steady alternation between tutti and solo parts. A kind of rondo form emerged, which, however, was more sophisticated than the traditional rondo, because each tutti return came in a different key, to return ultimately to the key of departure. Thus the laws of tonality were established structurally as well.

This idea was being enlarged upon in the concerto grosso, in which the contrasting solo part was taken over by a group of concertanti instruments. A late example is the *Concerto Grosso* by Barsanti (record 2, side 1, band 1), in which the concertante group consisted of one trumpet, two oboes, and timpani. This group opposed en bloc the ripieno of the strings. The formal scheme was enlarged. To the first movement was added a slow introduction, and the last movement appeared in Italian overture form, allegro–andante–allegro; but the three-movement division was maintained. Wind and percussion, instead of strings, came into use more as concertante groups, as can be seen also with Telemann and Handel.

Both solo concertos and concerti grossi were executed with the most consummate skill by Vivaldi, who was the first to infuse the solo part with motival ideas from the tutti sections. He also used the orchestra to express programmatic ideas. While he looked forward in his internal scheme, externally he turned to earlier Baroque ideas and approached the French concept.

Yet, orchestral music was never quite capable of superseding chamber music. Here Corelli proved to be the master who developed the style of the chamber sonata to the point where it became the basic scheme for such chamber composers as Geminiani, Locatelli, Porpora, and others. Corelli established the four-movement scheme, slow–fast–slow–fast, for the *sonata da chiesa*. He introduced fugal textures, mostly in the second movements, and worked out the most moving bel canto melodies for the third. This then became the style of the Italian sonata from Corelli onward.

The melodic line of the instruments, mainly the violin, was transferred to the harpsichord by Domenico Scarlatti. In doing so, Scarlatti relinquished all polyphonic ramifications. He was the first to embark upon a purely harmonic style. Even when he wrote fugally, which was seldom enough, his second voices moved only in parallels with the first; as a result, no independent polyphony was created. Scarlatti was also the first composer to introduce a new second theme into the sonata. By being the first truly harmonic, double thematic composer, he was the most modern composer of Baroque music. Being the initial link between the Baroque and Classicism, he recently became one of the most popular of all

Baroque composers. (A not dissimilar case may also be made for Vivaldi, whose work, though subtler and still more restrospective, has in its essentials a parallel quality.)

Couperin, in imitation of Corelli, introduced the sonata and orchestral concerto into France. But, with him, the concerti often developed into suites and expanded sonata forms (record 2, side 1, band 3, and side 2, band 1). It was only Leclair who mastered the Italian sonata style completely and thus could achieve a fusion of both styles in chamber music.

The essence of the French Baroque style lies in the harpsichord music, of which Couperin was the greatest master and which Rameau finally enlarged through daring harmonic experiments. These became the seminal points of the Rococo.

The German style is a style in itself when expressed in organ music through the chorale prelude. But chamber and orchestral music were subject to foreign influences, mainly the French. (For a very long time, Lully was considered the master of chamber music by the German musicians.) Telemann is the prime example of this tendency. He was the essential composer to bridge the gap between German Baroque and Rococo. His numerous suites were written in the spirit of the French orchestral works. Kuhnau was another composer who, although he adhered to the German polyphonic texture in his keyboard works, accepted the French idea of detailed program in his *Biblical Sonatas* (record 2, side 2, band 2).

The Italian influence is most felt in the orchestral music of J. J. Fux, whose suites combined southern melodiousness with northern contrapuntal austerity. A combined influence of French and Italian styles can be traced in another southern German master, Muffat.

The Italian influence was of far-reaching consequence in Handel, the German composer who was to become the leading spirit and symbol of late English Baroque music. Handel had gone to England as an Italian composer. He stayed there, and, although he never learned to speak English correctly, he absorbed a great deal of the English climate, the "pomp and circumstance" atmosphere to which he was to give such magnificent expression in his oratorios. He made use of various national styles in his music wherever he deemed it appropriate, but he never fused them into one big style. Handel's music was Italian music, or French music, or German music, as he needed it, but, to be sure, it was music created by a tremendous personality and a genius. In an era of strictly national music, he created the first big supernational—not to say international—body of work.

In his instrumental music—the trio sonatas, the organ concerti, and the concerti grossi—he modeled himself after Corelli. In his oratorios he strove for the monumental, the large performing body which required extravagant doublings. He was the first to write dynamic crescendi and decrescendi (in the *Chandos Anthems*), and in creating those huge blocks of music he seemed to hark back to the days of Monteverdi and Gabrieli. In him Italy extended her influence beyond her national boundaries to an important degree.

We find at the beginning of the Baroque period an overpowering musical personality in Monteverdi. We encounter at its end perhaps the greatest musical genius of all times, Johann Sebastian Bach. Fundamentally Bach was a German composer. The principle underlying his music was constructivist to the extent that occasionally one is tempted to subconscious mathematical speculations, as, for instance, in the famous *Passacaglia in C Minor,* whose twenty variations are constructed in strictest symmetry. But as Bukofzer pointed out, "Bach imbued the quasi-mathematical permutations of the mechanical patterns which appealed so strongly to Baroque speculation with visionary life and elevated what was at the time a mere vehicle for invention to an eternal work of art."

The password to Bach's music is construction and inspiration. In his gigantic polyphonic fantasies he always used the chorale as anchor. His themes were individually profiled; mostly they were linear and far removed from Vivaldi's triadic invention. His ornamentation was forever structural and not mannered, as in the French agréments. Toward the end of his life, as if to reassert once more his constructivist love, Bach returned to a close examination of the fugue in *The Art of the Fugue*. But for all his adherence to strict structure, Bach's inspirational powers were so great that hardly any two works are alike. As Kirnberger remarked, "He who knows a fugue by Bach knows really one only."

Bach's basic method of composition is nowhere clearer than in his treatment of text. In later Baroque music, there had taken place a kind of neutralization of the words. Often the same music was used for different texts. When musical symbolism was used to express literally a textual meaning, it was done in merely stereotyped fashion. The symbols were of a set order, but no fresh creations emanating from them illuminated the meaning of the words.

For Bach the words were form-giving. He demanded that his pupils, when playing a chorale, do so "according to the tenor of the words." His method of symbolic composition can be gleaned from the setting of the famous soprano aria "We Tremble and Stumble" from the *Cantata No. 105*, composed in 1725. There is no continuo instrument in this work; the bass line is given to the violas. This indicates the weakness of the spiritual ground; in addition, the accompaniment proceeds in short rhythmic patterns expressing the "trembling." Yet, in the finale of the cantata, when this idea recurs again in a grandiose summing up of the content of the entire work, the trembling accompaniment gradually changes into a firm and steady rhythmic figure, which, together with a firmly established bass and a strong melody, expresses unshakable faith.

Here then the musical figures are not literary in themselves, but take on an extramusical meaning only through their connection with the text. As the text changes, they change. They are not separate mannerisms, but comprehensible only in the larger context of the work in which they have become symbolic, poetic expressions. Bach's allegory is musical, and not literary.

This basic method of composing was in keeping with the German tradition; but it evolved to its last consequence in Bach. Foreign styles influenced him as well. Bach took a great deal from the Italians, as can be seen in the great number of transcriptions he made of Italian compositions, which he then bent to his own purpose.

He also absorbed numerous French influences. His courantes, for example, alternate in French and Italian style. In the Partitas and French Overture, the French influence is strongly manifest. His dance compositions extend into abstractions, and while they depend rhythmically on the dance meter, as a total work they have but little to do with the dance.

In Bach's clavier music we find influences of Froberger, which, stemming from Frescobaldi, point toward the Italian. However, it was through Couperin that the style came to Bach. Thus he absorbed into his basic German personality both the French and Italian styles and fused them. In doing so, he created, not a supranational style, but rather a style that was the supreme summing up of all the strands within the Baroque.

Bach's music is a codification of the Baroque. Even the high secular joy of southern Catholicism is wedded to the austere polyphony of northern Protestantism.

Bach was not an innovator, but a fulfiller. His music is essentially conservative. His impatient son, Johann Christian, described this conservatism in a derogatory manner by referring to his father as "the old wig" (*die alte Perücke*). It is a joke of history that the Italian "parucca" is the word that some believe to be the source of the term "Baroque."

Bach's music is at once the ultimate fulfillment and the final note of the Baroque. No further road leads from there. It was Rameau upon whom Gluck had to build the path which led into the Rococo and ultimately toward Classicism.

Bach's music is the best that the Baroque has to offer; indeed, it is probably the best that music has ever had to give.

5

THE ROCOCO
Exit and Opening

Bach died in 1750. That year is the symbolic closing of the Baroque period. Dates are not quite so easy for the Rococo. Its roots reach far into the French Baroque. Important decades overlap with the late decisive Baroque years. It is almost impossible to determine its end, for the boundary lines between the Rococo and Classicism are blurred. Yet, a vast, and not necessarily unimportant, body of music with a satisfactory community of stylistic characteristics is sufficient to consider the Rococo a definitive musical period. This body has clear Baroque qualities, on the one hand, and, at the same time, a number of properties which, if they do not yet belong to the age of Classicism, nevertheless point to it. Therefore, we must consider the Rococo to be the decisive connecting link between these two grand periods.

Such a view helps to determine the two chronological pillars of the Rococo, provided that one remembers that the dates are arbitrarily chosen. In 1724, Rameau published his *Pièces de clavecin,* which contained *Le Rappel des oiseaux, La Villageoise,* and *Les Tourbillons,* all pieces highly characteristic of the new era. In 1791, Mozart finished *The Magic Flute,* this ultimate mixture of Baroque and Rococo elements. It seems logical to take these two dates as boundary posts of the period. This is highly unorthodox, being in direct opposition to the theory that places the Rococo in the middle of the Baroque (at least in France) and calls the period after 1750 "pre-Classical" without any further definition. But the orthodox opinion only adds to the confusion. It tears Baroque into two and bypasses the historical dual role of the Rococo as the outgoing note of the Baroque and the signal of Classicism.

Between 1724 and 1790 there lie a number of disparate works. There are typical Baroque compositions, such as Bach's *The Art of the Fugue* (1748–1750) and Handel's *Messiah* (1742); one of the first classical operas, Gluck's *Iphigénie en Aulide* (1774); such classical symphonies as Haydn's *Trauersymphonie* (1772) and Mozart's *Haffner Symphony* (1782). However, there are also characteristic Rococo achievements, such as the works of Carl Philipp Emanuel Bach and the Mannheim School, the early Haydn, and Mozart.

Unless one keeps apart the Baroque and the Classical period from true Rococo, our dates create more confusion than clarity. Obviously, the Rococo is not a clearly defined period, but an intermingling of styles lying between Baroque and Classicism and leading from one to the other. It is this imprecision that characterizes the period most and makes it so charming, at the same time pointing up its secondary position. History is not always kind to pedants; and this is one instance in which it is absolutely cruel.

The roots of the Rococo go back to Lully. At that time, members of the court participated actively in the grand spectacles. Highborn dilettanti were in endless quest for entertainment. The desire for pleasure grew even stronger in the era of the regency following the death of Louis XIV in 1715 and reached its climax during the reign of Louis XV.

The name "Rococo" is a derivation from "rocaille," the artificially laid out rock gardens of Louis XV, so characteristic of the period.

Society was split into two classes. The higher class comprised the wealthy courtiers and aristocrats, who culturally mattered most.

The lower class was formed by the masses, exploited and poor, in a completely passive role. The Church, weakened through the dispute between Jansenists and Jesuits, contributed little from the cultural point of view. The aristocratic world of splendor was gay-hearted, eager for sensuous pleasures. The composers were employed by the court, a situation that did not change essentially until Mozart. Favorite forms of entertainment were idyls and pastorals. Music was frilly and programmatic, as in the works of the clavecinists Daquin and Clérambault. This kind of spirit, imbued with playfulness and fripperies and with external description only, remained with French music practically up to Debussy and Ravel.

Amorousness, elegance, and excessive adulation of woman as an object of erotic play characterize the era. We find the word *galant* appears for the first time to describe it all. Whatever had been decorative externally in the Baroque turns to internal decoration in the Rococo, a development to which the agréments bear witness. Music had become a game, and nothing was taken seriously. Marin Marais, a pupil of Lully, wrote a witty musical description of a gallstone operation. Guillemain and others imitated hunting scenes. It is this sort of superficial "naturalism" that led to Pergolesi's delightful opera *La serva padrona* and to Mozart's *Bastien und Bastienne*. Rousseau created a sensation with his call for a return to nature. His slight opera with a pseudo-rural setting, *Le devin du village*, was a fabulous success. At the same time, a call in favor of a return to Classicism, albeit a misunderstood one, gained importance. The engravings of Piranesi, the esthetic writings on Greek art by Winckelmann, and those by Lessing opposing Winckelmann's theory helped to shape the profile of the age. As unconditional absolutism developed into a more enlightened variety, especially with Prussia's emergence as a new power in the Seven Years' War, the ideas of Voltaire and Montesquieu, Burke and Hume, and the Encyclopedists gave the age a new face. There came to the fore an almost mystic belief in the power of human reason and a violent reaction against the church (Voltaire's "écrasez l'infame"). This prevented the music of the *galant* era from becoming stuck in the molasses of amours and fake nature idyls, despite its turning away from the strict rules of the Baroque and a great emphasis on the gay and sensuous. The affect of the senses in a new, individual, and nontraditional, universal Baroque sense gains in importance.

Sensibility (the French *sensibilité* and the German *Empfindsamkeit*) is the keyword. The general Baroque symbols have lost their value. They have given way to a direct personal affect which in each work is created anew.

The *style galant*, which developed from the time of Louis XV onward, combined Baroque and Rococo features (mostly in Rameau) and still wielded its influence in Mozart's later days. It is clearly recognizable from about 1720 onward. Primarily it is harmonic. The upper voice dominated and ruled over all others, which served to give it harmonic support. Counterpoint, if present at all, was only accidental. In the *Double Concerto for Clarinet and Bassoon* by Karl Stamitz, for example, the two concertanti instruments never play against each other, but run only in parallels; at best, they alternate in the presentation of thematic substance. This, however, was not considered imitation, because it did not result in a polyphonic juxtaposition of the two instruments (record 3, side 1, band 1). Such treatment was unthinkable in Baroque music, where the reason for the existence of two concertanti instruments was their mutual contrapuntal use.

The harmonic style was varied through what Mattheson calls *Brechung* (splitting up). It was a technique that was introduced originally when five or more parts of the vocal madrigal had to be contracted into a three-part instrumental composition by way of transcription. In this technique two voices did the work of one. Their melodic line was interrupted by a shift from the melody of one to that of the other. In the *style galant* this became a style element. A melody that ordinarily would have moved in quarter notes was now "broken" into eighth notes that combined the harmonic essence of two or more voices. The so-called Alberti bass was the final boiling down of this technique, which reduced a subtle harmonic motion to a nervous movement. Except in its primitive uses, the *Brechung* helped to underline the harmonic content without letting it become static.

The cadence was now the most important form-building element. When it came to a melodic standstill, it sounded occasionally like a sigh, an effect often sought after in the age of sensibility, and one liked to speak of "sighing cadences." This sort of treatment required a new dynamic approach. The cadence was expressive in itself, and its expressiveness was underlined by contrasted dynamics, which were constantly changing. They were more extreme than before and kept in step with the phrasing. The atmosphere was exaggerated, artificial, sentimental, and precious, but it was of a distinct style. The limits were set farther apart, and the tempo distinctions grew. All was written out in a detailed score so that the performer need not guess at what was requested of him.

When the terraced dynamics and the simple, straightforward phrasing disappeared, a formal organization emerged, which tied together thematic substances in clusters of a given number of bars. Thematic periodicity ensued. The theme was built on the basis of a number of motifs in a kind of motival pointillism. In the *Quintet* of Süssmayr the motifs make up the theme in sequential repetition (record 2, side 2, band 1). Gradually each motif is taken out of its thematic context and leads a life of its own. It was being varied, and the technique of splitting off the motifs in order to develop them individually came into being.

The embellishments took on a new function. In part they were pure frills. They appeared more frequently, but each was shorter. They participated in and contributed to the dissonance-consonance equilibrium. Quantz wrote: "Appoggiaturas in playing are not only a means of ornamentation, but are also a necessary thing. . . . In order that a melody appears galant, it must always have more consonances than dissonances. If many consonances appear in succession, and if, after several quick notes, a long consonance follows, the ear can easily become fatigued. The dissonances, therefore, must reawaken it from time to time. To this end the appoggiaturas can contribute much, because, if they stand before the third or sixth, counting from the fundamental tone, they become dissonances, namely fourth and seventh. However, they receive their proper resolution through the following note." In such a system nothing is left to the imagination of the performer; he is strictly bound by convention. Everything is prescribed, even the taste of the listener.

As early as 1713 Mattheson wrote an essay on "How an 'homme galant' may acquire a perfect understanding of the loftiness and majesty of noble music, form his taste accordingly. . . ." The words "loftiness," "majesty," and "noble" come from the Baroque vocabulary, but the "taste" (goût) and its prescribed formation pointed to a typical age of reason and Rococo conceit.

As soon as the lower voices began to perform the function of lending harmonic support to the uppermost voice, the use of the harpsichord as continuo instrument diminished. At first it was retained as a kind of relic, and in orchestral pieces it served the conductor as support in leading an instrumental group rather than as an integral part of the orchestration. Indeed, in the works of Starzer and Fasch we notice a deliberate omission of the continuo part. In the *Trio* of Haydn enough harmonic notes were allotted to the second violin and cello so that they, along with the melody part of the first violin, give a complete harmonic picture (record 3, side 1, band 2). A harpsichord may have been played along with the three instruments, but it was by no means essential in giving expression to what the composition had to say. From this technique eventually developed the string quartet and the typical chamber music of the Classical period.

The strict harmonic scheme (tonic-dominant juxtaposition of the large Bach fugues) determined the basic tonal structure of the Rococo sonata. Already in the keyboard sonatas of Domenico Scarlatti and in compositions of Galuppi a similar harmonic layout could be observed. In these works a polythematic structure was notable. These sonatas were influenced by the overtures to the Neapolitan operas and in turn influenced the overtures to the operas of Gluck, which eventually became independent symphonic pieces.

The use of two different themes, the second of which was in another key, was a feature taken over from the fugue. It was used methodically by Domenico Scarlatti and even more significantly by Pergolesi. In the latter's works, each secondary theme had a characteristic quite different from, and in contrast to, that of the primary theme. Pergolesi achieved this through the use of motival construction, which we have discussed in connection with Süssmayr. He was one of the first to lay the groundwork for the formal structure typical of Rococo instrumental music. The structure was further developed by Tartini and Veracini and reached a new climax in Giovanni Battista Sammartini, who added to the fast first movement in the above fashion. To the second movement he added the bel canto of the Baroque trio sonata, and, as a third and final movement of the Rococo sonata, he introduced the minuet.

The addition of the minuet as last movement had farreaching effects. It was a permanent feature in the symphonies of Boccherini. Later, the minuet was shifted to the second movement, as in the Haydn *Trio* (record 3, side 1, band 2). Finally, the form was expanded to four movements in the symphonies of the Austrian school.

The development of the Rococo as a secular Catholic movement (France, southern Germany, and Italy) was made apparent by the vigorous protests of the northern German composers against the inclusion of a fourth movement as "a sin against the spirit of the sinfonia." Yet, the Rococo eventually gained a foothold in northern countries as well, where Telemann, in many instrumental works, such as the *Tafelmusik*, formed a link between Baroque and Rococo.

With the cyclical form of the four movements, music arrived at a standard structure that was to dominate it in symphonic and chamber writing practically up to the Neo-Romanticism of the late Liszt and Richard Strauss. Quite schematically, the structure looked like this:

FIRST MOVEMENT	Sonata form, derived from the tonal relationship of *dux* and *comes* in the fugue, and first indicated by the dual themes of Domenico Scarlatti.
SECOND MOVEMENT	Aria form, derived from the instrumental bel canto style of the later days of the middle Baroque.
THIRD MOVEMENT	Minuet, taken into the structure from the dance suite and used at first as the last movement by Sammartini and Boccherini.
FOURTH MOVEMENT	Rondo form, orginally derived from the repetitive forms of the dance, but later, and more important, from the contrasting sections of ripieno and concertino in the concerti of Vivaldi.

Occasionally, one form replaced another. The rondo of the last movement might be displaced by another sonata form. Air and minuet might change places, but in all instances the movements stood in close key relationships to one another. Within themselves the movements were mostly tripartite. The sonata form consisted of exposition, development, and recapitulation; the air, of a front part, a middle section, and a shortened da capo of the front part.

The minuet was divided into the minuet proper, the trio, and the da capo of the minuet. For this the Baroque da capo technique provided the original inspiration. With one important difference, the da capos were rarely melodically varied. In the Baroque the variation of the da capo had been a matter of the performer's improvisational skill. It was based on the varied execution of the ornaments, slight tempo deviations, novel phrasing. When variations were added in Rococo music they were structural, not the results of subtle performance differences; they were the descendants of the variation technique that had been employed by the Baroque in the chaconne.

The cyclical forms, which began with Sammartini and led into the Austrian school, most notably Monn, Wagenseil, and eventually Dittersdorf, were by no means brought into play only in the symphonies, concerti, string quartets, and chamber sonatas. They were also used in the genres that characterize music as an entertainment medium: the divertimenti, serenades, and cassations. In them the influence of the Baroque suite was maintained through the addition of several dance sections to the movements of cyclical structure.

The cassation, a form favored by Haydn and Mozart, was known in its initial, rudimentary arrangement to Praetorius, who explained the derivation of the name from the German dialect expression *gassaten gehen* ("to promenade in the streets"): "It is an evening song with interspersed ritornelli, for three or more parts, performed while promenading on the street in the evening. At the universities they use it to serenade young girls." The serenades and cassations demonstrated the frequent practice of outdoor music.

The open-air performance required a higher dynamic level; consequently, the orchestra was enlarged and parts were doubled both at the unison and octave. The harpsichord disappeared. In its place a number of instruments served as harmonic aids, such as the woodwinds and horns. Haydn often wrote them ad libitum, which testifies to their primary harmonic use. In general, the texture was lightened; pedal harmonies were provided by horns and trumpets, rhythmical accentuation by timpani, and doublings by the woodwinds. A schematic type of orchestration developed that had lost some of Rameau's individualized Baroque color.

The typical orchestra of the time was large. The famous Mannheim orchestra consisted of eight first and eight second violins, four violas, two cellos, two double basses, three flutes, three oboes, two clarinets, four bassoons, and five horns. Leopold Mozart reported that the opera orchestra in Milan in 1770 had twenty-nine violins, six violas, two cellos, six basses, two each of flutes, oboes, bassoons, trumpets and harps, and four horns.

It has long been assumed that the Austrian school which was to become so important in further symphonic developments was strongly under the influence of Sammartini, especially as far as the string quartet was concerned. Myslivecek was the first to advance this opinion. Haydn, however, denied this. He had never esteemed Sammartini highly. He claimed Philipp Emanuel Bach as his chief authority. Obviously, the ideas were in the air and were made use of in many schools. The highly noteworthy influence in the Austrian school went back much further, that is, to J. J. Fux. His employment of strict polyphony in even the slightest dances left its mark on Haydn, whose music, for all its homophonic essence, never quite abandoned the contrapuntal treatment (record 3, side 1, band 2).

As soon as composers were no longer attached permanently to specific courts but traveled extensively, the influence of the Austrian school became felt all over Europe. At the same time an important group of composers gathered in Mannheim at the invitation of the Elector Karl Theodor (1724–1799), a cultured and energetic patron of the arts. Under the leadership of Johann Stamitz the Mannheim orchestra developed into the finest in Europe. Stamitz himself developed the symphony to a great extent. He introduced expressive crescendi and decrescendi. He developed the new motival technique and with it the so-called "Mannheim taste," which was calculated on surprise and through contrasts strove for a variety of effects rather than for the creation of one effect only in each movement, as had been the case in the Baroque. This technique was refined to greater detail by his son Karl, who, although perhaps the lesser composer of the two, worked out the principles so minutely and with such unrelenting consequence that Leopold Mozart complained about "the stereotyped mannerisms of the Mannheim goût." Riemann has pointed out the manifold advances of the Mannheim composers who, as he believes, were the inventors of the new style. But Guido Adler repudiates this by emphasizing the innovations of the Austrian school, that is, the development of chamber music apart from the symphonic music, the abandonment of the thorough bass, and the inclusion of the minuet as an additional movement of the symphony.

As a matter of fact, no single school or individual composer can be credited with all that was new. In addition to the Austrian and Mannheim schools, there were a number of other schools of perhaps lesser importance, such as the Berlin school with Philipp Emanuel Bach. Another was that of Graun and Quantz, who reintroduced the "folktune" into symphonic writing long before Haydn. They all flourished with the new style, and it is often hard to say whose influence had the most far-reaching effect.

Finally, these trends reached a climax in the work of Haydn and Mozart. With these two composers the decisive turn to Classicism took place. This, however, is the story of a new development quite remote from the days of the Baroque.

Out of the age of reason and the great search for enjoyment there had come a music which, in its formal balance and clarity, was clearly a child of its time. But what it had gained in lightness it had lost in subtlety and depth by giving up the direct effect and the profoundly involved contrapuntal texture of the Baroque. When Bach died in 1750, his music was virtually unknown in Europe. (*The Saint Matthew Passion* was discovered quite accidentally almost a century later by Mendelssohn.) Mozart had become acquainted with Bach's music only in his twenties (1782), but it made such a profound impression upon him that it left deep traces in his later music. This tremendously sensitive genius was aware of the shortcomings of the Rococo style, and, although he overcame these in many of his superb works, he always seemed to resent the loss of the polyphonic style. In many important works he very consciously strove for a return to it, as in the last movement of the *Jupiter Symphony*, the chorale prelude of the "Zwei Geharnischte" in the *Magic Flute*, and the *Adagio and Fugue* K 546 (record 3, side 2, band 2).

This re-introduction of the polyphonic style marks the beginning of a return to earlier days, a "neo" movement, albeit a small one. After that, the yearning for the polyphonic Baroque texture never ceased completely, Beethoven, Schumann, Brahms, Reger, Stravinsky, all revert to it occasionally.

Nor was Mozart the only one to express this longing of the Rococo days. The reintroduction of the suite form and repeated usage of contrapuntal techniques in later Rococo compositions were characteristic features of the new style.

And thus the cycle closed. From then on music was to explore other fields. The periods of the seventeenth and eighteenth centuries may occasionally be forgotten. But time and again their works penetrate anew the consciousness of the public.

PART TWO

6

A COMPARATIVE TIME SCHEDULE

Chronology Synchronized

In the following survey, the facts of history, general culture, and the arts are presented in chronological order. Only the most salient facts, as they create an overall picture of that Europe in which Baroque and Rococo music flourished, are enumerated. The periods are subdivided into five sections: 1580–1630, early Baroque; 1630–1680, middle Baroque; 1680–1725, late Baroque, first sector; 1725–1750, late Baroque, second sector, and Rococo, first sector; 1750–1790, Rococo, second sector.

A. 1580–1630

HISTORY. In 1588 King Philipp II of Spain sent his Armada on an abortive expedition against England. Queen Elizabeth of England reigned until 1603 and was succeeded by King James I, the first Stuart on the English throne. On the continent fighting broke out between the Reformation and the Counter-Reformation forces. In 1609 Rudolf II guaranteed religious freedom to the Bohemian Protestants. In the same year the Catholic League was founded by Maximilian I of Bavaria, opposing the Protestant Union. In 1618, the Thirty Years War began with a revolt of the Bohemian Protestants protesting against the violation of previously granted privileges. This war caused fearful damage to all of Germany.

In 1582, the Gregorian calendar was established, and the first public bank came into being in Venice in 1587, to be followed in 1609 by the bank of Amsterdam, the first central European bank. At about this time free trade as opposed to barter economy was firmly established. Nürnberg established the silver standard in 1621; Venice followed by dividing money into paper and coins. In Nürnberg a monthly newspaper appeared in 1599, and postal service was organized in 1615.

SCIENCE AND TECHNOLOGY. Galilei, who observed the movements of the pendulum (1583), invented the hydrostatic scale (1586), made gravitational experiments (1590), designed the precursor of the thermometer (1592), recognized the laws of inertia (1600) and made new planetary discoveries (1610), cited before the tribunal of the Inquisition (1615); Kepler's new conception of the cosmos (about 1619); the foundation of modern anatomy (1605); Bacon's measurement of the speed of sound (1600); the first logarithmic table by Napier (1614); circulation of blood in the human body investigated by Harvey (1618).

IDEAS. Bacon's writings (1597–1623); Böhme's *Mysterium magnum* (1623); Scaruffi's *Discourse about Money* (1582); the term "political economy" (1615).

LITERATURE. Tasso's *Gerusalemme liberata* (1581); de Montaigne's *Essais* (1588); Spenser's *Faerie Queen* (1590); the death of Marlowe (1593); Shakespeare plays; Jonson's *Volpone* (1605); Cervantes' *Don Quixote* (1605); Opitz's *Teutsche Poemata* (1624); *Hamlet* performed in Dresden (1626); works by Spanish dramatists Lope de Vega and Calderon de la Barca.

PAINTING. El Greco, Tintoretto, Bernini, Reni, Caravaggio; Rubens, Hals, van Dyck, Velasquez, Jan Brueghel the Elder, Rembrandt; Callot, Claude Lorrain.

ARCHITECTURE. Palais du Luxembourg finished by de Brosse (1620); St. Peter's in Rome, main building finished (1626), turrets and disposition of square taken over by Bernini (1629); Cathedral in Salzburg finished (1628); Hunting Chateau of Versailles finished (1626); Inigo Jones' projections for Whitehall (1619).

MUSIC. The first operatic attempts of the Camerata (around 1600); Monteverdi; initial attempts at thorough bass (Viadana); Giovanni Gabrieli's death (1612); Praetorius' *Syntagma Musicum* (1620); Schütz; Orlando Gibbons (dies in 1625).

B. 1630–1680

HISTORY. The Thirty Years War came to an end in 1648. The Westphalian peace treaty granted freedom of worship to the Protestants, the powers of the Emperor of the Holy Roman Empire were restricted. Various German principalities gained in importance, especially that of Brandenburg-Prussia under Friedrich Wilhelm (1640–1688). Austria developed into a major power. The repeated attacks of the Ottoman Empire were repelled in 1683, when beleaguered Vienna was spared Turkish occupation.

Under the guidance of Richelieu and Mazarin the powers of the French aristocracy were reduced, and the foundation to French absolutism was laid. When Louis XIV ascended the throne (1661), he reigned as absolute monarch. Mercantilism and state monopolies in manufacture, ideas of the French Minister of Finance, Colbert (1619–1683), laid the foundation of France's industrialization. Catholicism became French state religion (1682). To a lesser degree mercantilism gained ground in the German duchies and in Austria, where extensive systems of administration were developed.

In England, many Protestants left the country because of the King's Catholic favoritism. The Cromwellian revolt (Civil War 1642–1646) ended with the beheading of the Stuart King Charles I and the establishment of the Commonwealth. After the death of Cromwell and the resignation of his son and successor, the Stuart line was restored to power (1660). The parliamentary system developed (new parties, Whigs and Tories), and the habeas corpus acts were elaborated. The Anglican state religion was restored in 1662.

SCIENCE AND TECHNOLOGY. Cavalieri published *Geometria* (1635); "Laterna magica" invented by Kirchner (1646); beginning of comparative geography by Varenius (1650); air pressure demonstrated by Guericke (1654); microscopic anatomy initiated by Malpighi (1661); Boyle-Mariotte's law of gaseous pressure (1662); Newton's numerous discoveries; modern geology founded by Steno (1669); Leibniz' discovery of the electric spark (1687), establishment of infinitesimal calculation (1675).

IDEAS. The monism of Spinoza (1632–1677), the monad theory of Leibniz, and the rationalism of Descartes (1596–1650) the leading philosophies; anti-Jesuist doctrine of grace (1640) founded by Jansen; Hobbes' *Leviathan* (1651); Pascal turns from mathematics to religious philosophy (1656).

LITERATURE. Corneille's *Le Cid* (1636). Molière founds the "Illustre Theatre" (1643). Gryphius' satire on the Thirty Years War, *Horribilicribrifax* (1663). Dryden. Racine's *Andromache* (1667). Milton's *Paradise Lost* (1667). Lafontaine's *Fables* (1668). Grimmelshausen's *Simplicius* (1669). Bunyan's *Pilgrims' Progress* (1675).

PAINTING. The high periods of Rembrandt, Hals and Rubens. Pieter Brueghel the Younger, Ruisdael, Vermeer. Murillo, Rosa. Poussin, Le Brun.

ARCHITECTURE. Borromini and Bernini. Guarini finishes San Lorenzo in Turin (1666). Christopher Wren begins St. Paul's Cathedral in London (1672). Perrault finishes the Eastern facade of the Louvre (1667).

MUSIC. First public opera house in Venice (1637). Lully in France, Schütz in Germany. Development of the Sonata.

C. 1680–1725

HISTORY. Austria became a major power after defeating the Turks decisively in a number of wars under the leadership of Prince Eugene of Savoy. At the peace treaty of Passarowitz (1718) the Habsburg Empire reached its largest extension. Yet, in the War of the Spanish Succession (1701–1713–14), the first war embracing all Europe, with battles raging in Spain, Italy, Southern Germany, and the Netherlands and on the seas, the alliance between England, Holland, Austria, and several smaller states could only restore the equilibrium with her adversary, France, which was supported by the Wittelsbachs of Bavaria, in the peace of Utrecht (1713).

In England, King James II attempted Catholic restoration. In the "glorious revolution" (1688) William III of Orange became King of England. Through the acceptance of the Declaration of Rights (1689), a constitutional monarchy was established for the first time. Scotland and England were united to form Great Britain (1707), and the house of Hanover acceded to the British throne (1714). Mercantilism suffered a serious setback when Huguenots fled from France after the abrogation of the Tolerance Edict of Nantes in 1685. But by 1700 several large manufactures employing as many as a thousand workmen each had been founded. Hugenots imported into Germany many French manufacturing methods. In England, free-trade capitalism and expansion of Far Eastern trade began. The first savings bank was founded in 1698.

SCIENCE AND TECHNOLOGY. Pendulum clock constructed by Clement (1680); probability calculation (integral) by Bernouilli (around 1700); invention of the steam pot by Papin (1681); Newton's *Principis mathematics* (1687); wave theory of light published by Huygens (1690); mercury thermometer developed by Fahrenheit (1714); Foundation of modern acoustics by Sauveur (1700).

IDEAS. First universal history by Bossuet (1681); Locke's *Two Treatises of Government* (1689); Shaftesbury's *An Enquiry Concerning Virtue* (1699); Berkeley's *Principles of Human Knowledge* (1710); Bayle's *Dictionnaire* (1685–87); Vico's *De nostri temporis studiorum rations* (1709).

LITERATURE. Congreve's *Love for Love* (1694); works of Pope and Defoe; first appearance of the *Spectator* in 1711.

PAINTING. Watteau.

ARCHITECTURE. Versailles finished by Hardouin-Mansart (1688); the construction of Schönbrunn, summer residence of the Habsburgs begun by Fischer von Erlach (1694); the façade of St. Nicolaus in Prague finished by Dientzenhofer (1711); Lucas von Hildebrandt; the brothers Asam; Balthasar Neumann.

MUSIC. Corelli's first *Concerto grosso* (1680); Purcell's *Dido and Aeneas* (1689); Kuhnau's first keyboard sonatas (1696); the first Hammerklavier (1711); Handel to England (1712), writes *Water-music* (1714); Bach's *Brandenburg Concerti* (1721); Neapolitan operas by A. Scarlatti.

D. 1725–1750

HISTORY. In 1740 Charles VI died, and despite the "Pragmatic Sanction" of 1713, the accession of his daughter Maria Theresia to the Austrian throne was opposed by Prussia. This led to the War of the Austrian Succession (1740–1748), in which Austria ceded Silesia to Prussia, which in turn emerged as one of the leading European powers after having centralized its administration and created a large army under its ruler Frederick William I. His son, Frederick the Great, established firmly the power of Prussia after his accession to the throne in 1740.

In France, a regency was set up after the death of Louis XIV in 1715, which continued the absolutist reign on behalf of the late king's five-year-old son Louis XV, despite a state bankruptcy which was the consequence of the extensive use of paper money, a system developed by the Scot John Law. All financial reforms were obstructed by the clergy and high aristocracy.

SCIENCE AND TECHNOLOGY. Exact measuring of blood pressure by Hales (1726); discovery of the aberration of light by Bradley (1728); stereotypography invented by Ged (1729); Boerhaave's classic *Elementa Chemiae* (1732); Euler's *Mechanica* (1736); Linné's natural system of living creatures in *Systema naturae* (1735); the first weaving machine developed by Wyatt (1738); Benjamin Franklin's experiments with electricity (1742); first electrical condenser (1745); electrotheraphy begun around 1750; first book on statistical theory by Archewall (1749); sailing through Bering Strait (1728).

IDEAS. Rise of Freemasonry; Montesquieu's writings; Voltaire's writings; Frederick the Great, still crown prince, writes his *Anti-Machiavell* (1739), a state philosophy of enlightened absolutism; Hume's *On Human Nature* (1739).

LITERATURE. Swift's *Gulliver's Travels* (1726); writings of Pope; Prévost's *Manon Lescaut* (1731); Merivaux's *Les fausses confidences* (1737); French classical drama imitated by German theater (Gottsched's *Cato,* 1732); Fielding's *Joseph Andrews* and *Tom Jones* (1749); Richardson's *Clarisea* (1748): the new commedia dell'arte by Goldoni and Gozzi; Klopstock's *Messiah* (1748).

PAINTING. Tiepolo; Canaletto; Hogarth; Boucher.

ARCHITECTURE. St. Nepomuk Church in Munich finished by brothers Asam (1733); Potsdam Palace (1744) and Sans Souci Palace near Potsdam (1747) both built by Knobelsdorff; Würzburg Residence by Neumann finished (1744).

MUSIC. Domenico Scarlatti; Bach's *St. Matthew Passion* (1729); Pergolesi's *La serva padrona* (1733); Handel's *Twelve Concerti Grossi* (1739); Bach's *Goldberg Variations* (1742); Johann Stamitz appointed *Kapellmeister* at Mannheim (1745).

E. 1750–1790

HISTORY. The rivalry between Austria and Prussia flared up again in the Seven Years War (1756–1763), which involved a good part of Germany, France, and even England (in conflicts over colonies, such as Canada), but ended with an even stronger Prussia. German nationalism began to rise. In Germany dualism flourished, with Prussia and Austria alternately in the lead. In both countries there was an era of enlightened absolutism. In Prussia, interior colonization, rational methods in agriculture, increasing bureaucracy, religious freedom, and a juridical system based on equality before law developed. Similar developments took place in Austria, with the exception of religious freedom. Under Joseph II there were far-reaching reforms (1781): religious tolerance; abolition of serfdom. In England extensive industrialization and world-wide trade developed. The American Revolution took place (1775–1783).

SCIENCE AND TECHNOLOGY. Lightning rod invented by Franklin (1752); comprehensive physiology published by Haller (1757); geometrical projections by Lambert (1759); hydrogen discovered by Cavendish (1766); Euler's *Algebra* (1766); first modern textile factory in Nottingham (1769). Watt invents the steam engine (1769); modern chemistry founded by Lavoisier (1774); ammonia and oxygen discovered by Priestley (1774). "Electrophor" constructed by Volta (1775); planet Uranus discovered by Herschel (1781); the "figures" of sound in bodies of even (sound) vibration discovered by Chlodni (1787); exploration of Australia, New Zealand, South Seas, Alaska by Cook.

IDEAS. Rousseau's *Discours sur les sciences et les arts* (1750); Jonson's *Dictionary of the English Language* (1754); French Encyclopedia (1751–1780) with cooperation of Diderot, d'Alembert, Voltaire, Rousseau; Winckelmann's *Thoughts on the Imitation of the Greek Works in Painting and Sculpture* (1755); Hume's *Natural History of Religion* (1755); Burke's A *Philosophical Inquiry* and Voltaire's *Essai sur les moeurs et l'esprit des nations* (1756); Voltaire's *Candide* (1759); Lessing's *Laokoon* (1766); Moses

Mendelssohn's *Phaidon* (1767); Herder's *On the Origin of Language* (1772); Lavater's *Physiognomic Fragments* (1775); new pedagogy by Pestalozzi (1780); Kant's *Critique of Pure Reason* (1781) and *Critique of Practical Reason* (1788).

LITERATURE. Casanova's *Memoirs* (1756); Stern's *Tristram Shandy* (1760 to 1767); Rousseau's *La nouvelle Héloïse* (1761); Goldsmith's *The Vicar of Wakefield* (1766); works of Lessing, the young Goethe, and Schiller; Goethe's *Werther* (1774); Beaumarchais' *Le barbier de Seville* (1775); Sheridan's *The Critic* (1779).

PAINTING. Piranesi, Guardi, Goya; Greuze, Fragonard; Reynolds, Gainsborough.

ARCHITECTURE. The Rococo Theatre in the Munich residence (1750), built by Cuvilliés.

MUSIC. Rousseau's *Le devin du village* (1752); Mozart's *Bastien und Bastienne* (1768); Dittersdorf's *Doktor und Apotheker* (1786); works by Mozart and Haydn.

7

THE MUSICAL EXAMPLES

An Educational Concert

The recorded musical examples were selected for didactic purposes to illuminate best the periods under discussion. Whether small or large, each represents a complete work. The purpose of the order of the examples is to give the most pleasure in listening. While, thus, the recorded examples can, and should, be listened to in conjunction with the text, they can also be enjoyed simply as entertainment. Each record represents a small concert and, aside from any educational objective, should provide a pleasant musical diversion.

There is an overall title for each record. Above and beyond its significance, the items are exemplary of a variety of facets.

Record 1: *The Sound of Baroque*
Side 1
Band 1 Johann Pezel:

Turmmusik in B Flat Major for Two Trumpets and Three Trombones

Intrada–Allemande–Courante–Sarabande–Bal

The *Stadtpfeifer* were called upon for all sorts of occasions, such as indication of the hours, special signals, ceremonial events. Pezel composed a great number of pieces, apt for any of these occasions, chiefly in dance form, of which seventy-six are extant. They were published in 1685 in parts. Probably at important events several were performed together in a primitive kind of suite. Five were selected for this recording in a suite arrangement which is likely to approximate that of the composer's time. With the exception of the *Intrada,* the pieces are dances in two part form; the first part is always repeated. Allemande and bal are in double time; courante and sarabande are in triple time. The intrada is a free double form built on a signal.

The parts were written for brass, which points to the outdoor use of the composition. The first edition of the parts of the year 1685 carries the following inscription: Johannis Pezelii Fünff-stimmigte blasende Music, bestehend in Intraden, Allemanden, Balleten, Courenten und Giguen, als zweyen Cornetten und dreyen Trombonen.

Band 2 Henry Purcell:
A New Ground in E Minor for Harpsichord

This piece, taken from the harpsichord collection *Musick's Handmaid,* published in 1689, features a favorite variation form which is basically the same as the ciaconna and passacaglia. Over the same bass of three measures, which is the essential theme, the upper voice executes ten variations. The bass figure initiates a succession of the broken chords of E minor, B major–minor, A major–minor, two times E minor–B major, and finally E minor. This establishes a chromatic downward scale of *e, d* sharp, *d* natural, *c* sharp, *c* natural, *b* in the first half, and a diatonic downward scale of *b, a, g, f* sharp, *e* in the second half of the theme. The varying voice breaks into three separate sections in each variation, each of them taking up one measure. Thus, a contrast of two one-and-a-half-measure groups in the bass and three one-measure groups in the descant ensues. Furthermore, variations three and four repeat variations one and two, and variations eight, nine, and ten repeat variations five, six, and seven. This makes for an expanding form; double variation is followed by triple variation, a highly constructivist principle.

Band 3 J. S. Bach:
Prelude in E Flat Minor for Clavichord, from *The Well-tempered Clavier*, vol. I, BWV 583

The preludes and fugues of the *Well-tempered Clavier*, whose first part dates from 1722, can be—and most probably also were—performed on any number of keyboard instruments. This "E Flat Minor Prelude," however, seems predestined for the clavichord, whose peculiar vibrato sustaining qualities allow the sound of the harmonies to endure. This feature is important in a composition in which the functional harmony changes from bar to bar only in thirty-one out of forty measures. Bach's sensitive monolinear, harmonic writing, with the exception of seven contrapuntal bars lying exactly in the middle of the piece, depends upon the slow and gradual shift of the harmony over a triadic motif. The considerably lower volume of tone of which the clavichord is capable in comparison with the harpsichord gives the composition a peculiar sense of intimacy.

Band 4 Robert de Visée:
Prélude and Bourrée in D Minor for Guitar

These two selections are taken from the first edition of a variety of guitar pieces published in 1686. From this the performer always chose a few to his taste for presentation in loose suite form. The guitar is employed as an instrument of entertainment which was one of its principal functions. The simple, two-part "Bourrée," which is introduced by a rhythmical "Prélude," is chiefly harmonic.

Band 5 Johann Jakob Froberger:
Ricercare in C Minor for Organ

This early precursor of the fugue stems from a collected edition printed in 1693. It was probably written around the middle of the seventeenth century. It is divided into three distinct sections. In the first, the simple triadic theme, alternating in tonic and dominant form, is brought in traditionally by the four voices from bass to soprano. In the second part, the bass introduces it in its dominant form. It is imitated by the soprano in the tonic form and then by the alto again in the tonic form. The tenor, which was left out here, is the only voice to render the theme in the dominant form in the last part, which also constitutes the finale.

Band 6 Johann Caspar Kerll:
Capriccio Cucu in G Major for Harpsichord

Written in 1669, this short piece indulges in a favorite Baroque pastime. It imitates the call of the cuckoo by basing the entire form upon the minor third of that call, which is presented in a variety of harmonic guises. Through the registration possibilities of the harpsichord a particularly plastic picture unfolds.

Band 7 Johann David Heinichen:
Trio Sonata in G Major for Recorder, Oboe d'Amore, Viola da Gamba and Harpsichord

Andante–Allegro–Largo–Allergo

This heretofore unpublished sonata (the original manuscript is in the Hesse State Library at Darmstadt) is typical of the late Baroque *sonata da camera* form in its formal scheme slow–fast–slow–fast. The two upper-melody instruments stand in contrapuntal relationship to each other. The bass is the harmonic foundation and has little melodic motion of its own. The first movement in double time and the third movement in triple time are extensive ariosos. The motion is more stately in the third movement, while the first indulges in rhythmic elaboration of the melody. The second and fourth movements have two-part structures. Differentiation is provided by the double time of the second, and the triple time of the fourth in dance pattern. The execution of the work on the typical Baroque instruments makes this not only a significant specimen of the genre, but also offers a characteristic Baroque sound.

Band 8 J. S. Bach:
Prelude in C Minor for Lute, BWV 999

This piece probably written around 1720 in Köthen shows the influence of clavier music in the use of two voices against each other.

It was a common practice to employ similar techniques on lutes and claviers (see also next selection).

Band 9 Jean Baptiste Henri d'Anglebert:
Prélude in G Minor for Virginal

The "Prélude," written in 1689, shows the reverse trend from above. Here the clavier instrument appropriates the arpeggio techniques of the lute. This monolithic thematic approach requires one type of sound only, a purpose which is served well by the one-manual virginal. At this point it may be well to remember that both the virginal and the clavichord are table instruments; that is, unlike the harpsichord, which in its outward appearance is contructed in the manner of the modern piano, standing on three legs, both the virginal and the clavichord are simple boxes, which have to be placed on a table and which have no large sounding board, as have the harpsichord and the piano. Their limited resonance makes them ideal vehicles for house music.

Band 10 J. S. Bach:
Duetto I in E Minor for Clavichord, from the *Clavierübung, Third Part*, BWV 802

Written around 1739, the duets of the third part of the *Clavierübung*, this huge work of Bach for a variety of keyboard instruments, but mainly the organ, were definitely meant for either clavichord or harpsichord. In the first duet the downward stepping succession of chromatic tones—*e*, *d* sharp, *d* natural, *c* sharp, *c* natural, and *b*—and their transpositions are the basic formal element. They appear alternatingly in upper and lower voice; developing a form that resembles the ciaconna. The dual linearity is brought out with uncommon clarity by the clavichord, which thus shows another of its characteristics, making it an important implement in the execution of simpler polyphonic studies.

Side 2
Band 1 Giovanni Battista Vitali:
Sonata a Tre in D Minor for Strings and Organ

Allegro–Grave–Allegro–Vivace

This sonata, published first in 1667, is one of the earliest examples of the *sonata da chiesa*. The succession of fast—slow—fast—fast movements is atypical but further proof of how unstereotyped the earlier Baroque specimens are. The first movement, built on the initial theme, which is repeated several times in imitation by the two melodic voices, falls into two parts. The second movement consists of a steplike succession of harmonies with only the bass providing motion. After two measures of a slow introduction, which functions as a kind of transition, the third movement presents a theme in which the melody voices run mostly in parallels. A similar technique, though formally more extended, is also followed in the last movement. The last two movements make occasional use of syncopation, which points toward a dance influence. Harmonically, the work is still of modal conception. Each movement begins in D minor and ends in D major, with harmonies never reaching beyond the subdominant and dominant regions. In keeping with the style of the times, the melody voices are presented by a group of violins. The organ is the continuo instrument.

Band 2 Claudio Merulo:
Toccata in the Fourth Mode for Harpsichord

This toccata (the word means "composition for keyboard instruments") was probably written around 1580. Merulo may have performed it on the organ, but performance on the harpsichord is just as likely. Extensive use is made of modality, but recurring leading tones contain a faint hint of future tonality. Melodically, the piece adheres to the recitative style. Counterpoint in the later, conventional sense is absent; the leading voice is simple, with the countervoice executed in the recitative manner. This treatment occasionally gives the piece the appearance of a set of variations, which, however, is not its primary purpose. Nevertheless, the groundwork for such a future technique is laid here.

Band 3 Georg Philipp Telemann:
Sonata in G Minor for Flute, Cello, and Harpsichord

Adagio–(Adagio)–Vivace–Grave–Allegro

During Telemann's lifetime, a number of solo sonatas were published in which the composer wrote out in detail the ornamentations in the slow movements. Thus, an exact indication as to how the composer wished the embellishments executed is given. In this recording of one of twelve sonatas written prior to 1728, the first movement is played simply as printed without any ornaments. Then the movement is executed with all the ornaments as written out by Telemann. The listener is afforded a fine opportunity to follow the general principle of ornamentation. All held notes are embellished. The even motion of eighths is ornamented through a dissolution into sixteenth and thirty-second notes. An even sixteenth motion is made more interesting by being converted into dotted French rhythm. Formally, the work follows the scheme slow–fast–slow–fast; but the movements in parallel tempos are distinguished through time variants. The first movement is in 4/4 time, and the third, in 3/2; the second movement is in 6/8 time, and the last, in 2/4. The bass line is more than a harmonic ground: it is practically a melody voice. As such, it indulges in a great deal of imitation in the third movement.

Band 4 Peter Philips:
Amarilli di Julio Romano in G for Harpsichord

This work, probably written around 1620, is one of the earliest forms of structural variation. It uses for its theme a popular vocal canzone, probably composed by Caccini. The theme falls into two distinct parts, the second being a varied repetition of the first. In the second half of the composition occurs the actual variation technique. The theme is alternately expanded and contracted. Small sections are elaborated upon and the repetition of the variation is then a melodic elaboration of the variation itself. Thus, we have something that resembles a Chinese puzzle: theme, theme repeated with melodic elaboration, variation of theme, variation repeated with melodic elaboration upon it.

Band 5 Georg Friedrich Kaufmann:
Chorale Prelude on Nun danket alle Gott in F Major for Organ

This typical simple German chorale prelude, was probably written around 1700. The bass and middle voice follow a steady motion in eighth notes, a diminished and reversed variation of the original chorale melody. The variation is elaborated upon in twelve measures before the first strophe of the chorale itself enters in the uppermost voice. There are no larger interludes between the strophes of the chorale; there is simply a continuance of the motion while the cadential note of the chorale is held.

Band 6 John Mundy:
Fantasia for Harpsichord

This piece from around 1620 is an example of strictest program music. Outdoor events are described in alternating sections. Unlike the Kerll "Capriccio" (record 1, side 1, band 6), which gives an impression based upon the motival exploitation of the bird call, and the Kuhnau "Sonata" (record 2, side 2, band 2), which is an internal presentation of a dramatic event, the "Fantasia" is an impressionistic moment-by-moment description of a storm. The composer has inserted in the various sections the following descriptive headings, which determine the structure of the piece: (1) Faire wether; (2) Lightning–Thunder; (3) Calme wether; (4) Lightning–Thunder; (5) Faire wether; (6) Lightning; (7) Faire wether; (8) Lightning–Thunder; (9) A cleare Day. To modern ears, used to the heartier *Alpensymphonie* of Richard Strauss, this piece may seem feeble and primitive; but to Baroque audiences it had a real, and possibly terrifying, meaning, which gives us an interesting idea of the dynamics to which that public was accustomed.

Record 2: The Large Forms of Baroque
Side 1
Band 1 Francesco Barsanti:
Concerto Grosso in D Major, Op. 3, No. 10, for Orchestra

I. Adagio–Allegro; II. Largo; III. Allegro–Andantino–Allegro

This concerto grosso, written in 1742, is a late example of the genre. As such it demonstrates its most advanced features. The concertanti instruments are two oboes (which are used for a long stretch as one instrument by running constantly in parallels), one trumpet, and the timpani that give rhythmic accentuation. By doing so on the dominant-tonic alternations, they reaffirm tonality most strongly. The ripieno body consists of a full string orchestra. The continuo is executed on the harpsichord.

This is the formal scheme. First movement: an adagio introduction of a broad theme by the orchestra, then first bar imitated by the concertanti. This principle is repeated at first in the mediant and then in the dominant key; both times the ripieno imitation is extended to two bars. After this, the allegro: a double theme in the ripieno, one part brought in by the first violins and imitated by the seconds; the other part brought in by the bass and imitated by the violas. This gives the orchestra an opportunity to develop the idea in a constant weaving of imitations for twenty-four bars. Then, the concertanti take over the theme in canonic imitation between trumpet on one side and oboes on the other, with timpani rhythmically accentuating it. After this the imitation spreads out between trumpet, first oboe, and second oboe. Now there comes an imitative interlude on the same substance in the ripieno, followed by the concertanti with first oboe in the melodic lead, occasional second oboe imitation, and only rhythmic accentuation by trumpet and timpani, with accentuated accompaniment from the ripieno. A return to the initial scheme of ripieno—concertino with combined coda closes the movement.

Thus, the movement falls into three parts, the exposition in both ripieno and concertino, the imitative interludes, and the return to the initial statement.

The second movement, largo, is a bel canto aria for the strings alone. The concertante character has disappeared here. It returns in the third movement, which is a summing up of the first two movements. The substance lies in the ripieno, but the concertanti reinforce it through rhythmical accentuation without independent melodic motion. The form is that of the Neapolitan overture: two allegros framing an andantino for strings only.

Band 2 Antonio Vivaldi:
Concerto in C Minor ("Il Sospetto"), for Violin and Orchestra, F. I, No. 2 (P. 419)

Allegro–Andante–Allegro–(Harmonic Structure)

In all probability this is one of the later concerti from around 1740. The solo concerto technique is completely developed. After the initial tutti the solo instrument begins with its own theme, which has its origin in one of the tutti passages. Then the tutti theme follows. Again there are a short solo interlude and the tutti theme, a long solo exposition and a tutti coda. Thus, extended solo sections with their own distinctive material are encircled by the original tutti thematic substance.

The second movement is a cantilena for the tutti only. Violas, cellos, and basses play the bass line in unison and all the violins play the melody. There are no harmonic fill-ins indicated.

The third movement follows the concerto scheme of the first. The initial entrance of the solo instrument is an elaboration of a harmonic idea. We have appended the harmonic structure of the entire passage. It should be compared with the first entrance of the solo violin. The violin presents only the chords in extensive figuration. This kind of harmonic ornamentation is typical not only of Vivaldi's concerto technique but also of much harmonic elaboration in later Baroque compositions.

Band 3 François Couperin:
Les Nations. Sonates et Suites de Symphonies. Premier Ordre: La Française. In E Minor, for orchestra, Part I

In 1692, Couperin had written several trio sonatas under the influence of Lully and Corelli. One of these trio sonatas forms the first part of this suite. It consists of a number of sections. They alternate in tempo—slow–fast–slow–fast—and conclude with an air which, after a moderate introduction, winds up in fast tempo.

Side 2
Band 1 François Couperin:
La Française, Part II

In 1726, Couperin added to this trio sonata a second part consisting of a number of dances. This was done so skillfully that an entirely new composition emerged out of both parts. The first part (the original trio sonata) is a grand introduction to the succession of dances in the second part: allemande, two courantes in A–B–A form, sarabande, and gigue. Here, the dance series is interrupted by a weighty "Chaconne ou Passacaille." Then, the dance suite is taken up again by a succession of gavotte and minuet. Thus, a large structure is created, which, through the addition of the chaconne, makes the slow introduction logical. We see here in one composition how the large suite came into being and ended in a coherent symphonic form.

Band 2 Johann Kuhnau:
Sonata in G Minor from Six Biblical Sonatas for Harpsichord

In 1700, Kuhnau published a set of six sonatas, written on biblical themes. He endowed each of them with extended descriptive notes and prefaced them with an apologia which he apparently deemed necessary, although he stated quite correctly, "I am not the first to have happened upon such inventions, unless the famous Froberger's and other excellent composers' various *Batailles*, *Waterfalls*, and *Tombeaus* are quite ignored."

But he was the first to go beyond a merely sonic description such as we saw in the Mundy *Fantasia* (record I, side 2, band 6). He endows his large three movements with the spirit rather than the noise of the biblical story. Thus, he offers the listener a picture of an idea through a firmly established musical structure. In this sense he is the direct forerunner of Berlioz, Liszt, and Strauss, and certainly not the imitator of the clavecinists.

The second sonata shows a grandiose, nearly antique concept. Its title is "Saul malinconico e trastullato per mezzo della musica" ("The melancholy of Saul is cured by music"). The work falls into three movements: "La tristezza ed il furore del Re" ("The King's sadness and his fury"), a large preparatory movement which makes extensive use of the recitative and rubato styles; "La Canzona refrigerativa dell'arpa di Davide" ("David's refreshing song on the harp"), a sort of burlesca in dance motion where the harpsichord is used in imitation of the harp; and, finally, "L'animo tranquillo e contente di Saulo" ("The quiet and contented spirit of Saul"), a French-style piece built on one rhythmical figure.

Record 3 The Rococo
Side 1
Band 1 Karl Philipp Stamitz:
Concerto in B Flat Major for Clarinet, Bassoon, and Orchestra

Allegro Moderato–Andante Moderato–Rondo

In all probability this work dates from around 1775. It is practically a solo concerto. The two concertanti instruments act as one instrumental block and their duality contributes only to a change of color. Thus, for analytical purposes they can be considered one instrument, a practice quite common to the harmonic style of the late Rococo.

The form is that of the early symphony-concerto. The orchestra brings in the exposition with first theme, secondary theme in the dominant key, and short codetta. This section is repeated and elaborated upon by the concertanti instruments. A short development section and a shortened recapitulation with extended cadenza in the final coda follow.

We have here the perfect early concerto scheme. It is interesting that no detailed motival technique occurs. Each theme is built in several sections, and, except for the runs in the solo instruments, these sections are invariably kept intact.

The second and third movements are elaborate aria and short rondo forms, respectively. The cadenzas in both the first and last movements are by the composer, and they are rather extensive. In the last movement there is a cadenza before each new rondo section; thus it fulfills a structural role, which it loses in the later development of the concerto genre.

Band 2 Joseph Haydn:
Trio in G Major for Two Violins and Bass (Cello), Hob. V, G 3

Moderato–Tempo di Menuetto–Allegro

This trio was composed around 1760, if not earlier; certainly before Haydn's Esterhazy employment. As a work of transition, it is most revealing. Two facets tie it to the Baroque; the two descant voices are high up while the bass remains below, and there is an occasional imitative counterpoint, such as in the repetition of the initial theme, the J. J. Fux influence. Four facets point up its Rococo essence: a diminutive development section in the first (miniature sonata form) movement; a simple minuet without any tripartite structure (there is no trio as middle section); a simple dance as last movement; finally, the employment of the lower two voices as harmony fillers against the uppermost voice, rendering the use of a continuo superfluous.

Side 2
Band 1 Franz Xaver Süssmayr:
Quintetto in D Major for Flute, Oboe, Violin, Viola and Cello

Allegro con Brio–Adagio–Rondo: Allegretto

If internal evidence can be relied upon, then this work must have been written around 1791, for the last movement shows definite thematic influence of *The Magic Flute*. Possibly, this takes it out of the Rococo sphere. On the other hand, the unusual instrumental combination and rather elementary structure of the final rondo show it to be the work of an earlier period. However, what makes it interesting, more than the fact that it was written by Mozart's most gifted pupil, is the motival treatment in the first movement—the standard sonata form. The composer splits off three eighth notes on the same pitch as a recurring motif. Not only does he develop this idea within the primary theme, but also he uses it as an accompaniment to the secondary theme. We have here the beginnings of the classical technique. However, it is still tied to Rococo simplicity as witnessed in the quite straightforward aria form of the second movement, which, over a rather primitive and monotonous accompaniment, makes no attempt at elaboration.

Band 2 Wolfgang Amadeus Mozart:
Adagio and Fugue in C Minor for String Orchestra, K. 546

This is Mozart's return to the verities of the Baroque. In 1783, under the impression of the Bach fugues, he wrote the fugue for two pianos. Four years later, he set it out for string orchestra and, in the manner of the preludes and fugues in the *Well-Tempered Clavier*, prefaced it with the "Adagio." The composition, quite in the monumental style of Bach, departs in no instance from the general scheme of such works in the late Baroque.

8

COMPOSERS' BIOGRAPHIES

A Capsule View

The composers whose biographies are detailed here in brief are those mentioned in the text. They are singled out not necessarily for their importance but because they serve to illustrate a point in the narrative. Obviously a great number of important composers are missing.

AGAZZARI, AGOSTINO (1578–1640)
Of a noble family, Agazzari was in the service of Emperor Matthias. Later he went to Rome, where he became maestro di cappella at the Seminario Romano and at the church of Sant'Apollinare. Finally, he returned to his birthplace, Siena, where he held a similar post at the cathedral. A close friend of Viadana, he expounded on the thorough bass theory in an essay "Del suonare il basso sopra tutti gli stromenti e del uso loro nel concerto" (1607).

ALBERTI, DOMENICO (1710–1740)
Known in his lifetime chiefly for being an excellent singer and harpsichordist, Alberti was not necessarily the inventor of the "Alberti bass," but came to be associated with it through excessive and prominent employment of this technique in his sonatas, some of which were published by Walsh in London.

D'ANGLEBERT, JEAN-HENRI (1635–1691)
Organist to the Duke of Orléans and later successor to his teacher Chambonnières as clavecinist to Louis XIV, he published a table of *agréments*.

ARTUSI, GIOVANNI MARIA (1540–1613)
As canon of San Salvatore in Bologna, Artusi used his scholarship to oppose the "new music" of Monteverdi, chiefly in his book *L'Artusi, ovvero delle imperfettioni della musica moderna* (1600 and 1603).

BACH, CARL PHILIPP EMANUEL (1714–1788)
The second son of Johann Sebastian's first marriage and a godson of Telemann, Carl Philipp Emanuel was appointed harpsichordist at the court of Frederick the Great. In 1767, he left for Hamburg, where he became Telemann's successor at the Johanneum. Since he was one of the first Rococo composers, his influence was also acknowledged by Haydn and Mozart. Of great importance was his book *Versuch über die wahre Art das Klavier zu spielen,* which laid down many esthetic principles of the Rococo.

BACH, JOHANN CHRISTIAN (1735–1782)
At the age of nineteen, Johann Christian, the youngest son of Johann Sebastian's second marriage, also known as the "London" Bach, left for Italy to study with Padre Martini at Bologna. There he became a Roman Catholic. Several of his operas were produced in Italy. In 1762, he settled in London, achieving high esteem and much success with the production of his operas. Mozart visited him and came under the influence of his symphonic music, which is highly significant of the Rococo style.

BACH, JOHANN SEBASTIAN (1685–1750)
The important stations in Johann Sebastian Bach's life are: 1703–1707 organist at Arnstadt, from there visit to Lübeck and possibly some lessons with Buxtehude; marries his cousin Maria Barbara; 1707–8 organist in Mühlhausen; 1708–1717 Weimar, organist first, and then Konzertmeister; 1717–1723: Köthen, conductor of the court orchestra. After the death of his wife, he married Anna Magdalena (1721). In 1723, Bach was appointed cantor of the Thomasschule in Leipzig as successor of Kuhnau, after Telemann and Graupner, who had been chosen first, declined the post. In this post he spent the rest of his life. From Leipzig he made his celebrated visit to Frederick the Great in Potsdam.

BARSANTI, FRANCESCO (1690–?)
An Italian composer who went to England to study with Geminiani, Barsanti played as flautist first in London, then for several years in Edinburgh. He spent the last years of his life in London again, where he worked as violist in the opera orchestra and at Vauxhall Gardens. He probably died before 1776.

BIBER, HEINRICH IGNAZ VON (1644–1704)
This Bohemian-born composer attained highest esteem as a violin virtuoso at the court of the Archbishop of Salzburg, where he spent all his life as high steward and conductor. Biber was one of the first of the German composers to exploit the technical possibilities of the violin, going so far as to invent the *scordatura*, new kind of tuning for special effects.

BOCCHERINI, LUIGI (1743–1805)
Famous as a virtuoso on the cello, Boccherini spent most of his early years traveling and concertizing. From 1786 to 1797 he was in Berlin as court composer to Frederick William II. After that, he spent the remaining years of his life in Madrid, first under the patronage of Lucien Bonaparte, French ambassador to Madrid, but later, toward the end of his life, in abject poverty. During his life he wrote 467 instrumental compositions, of which the symphonies and chamber works (quintets, quartets, and trios) are of the greatest interest.

BONONCINI, GIOVANNI (1670–1755)
A cellist, first in Bologna, then in Rome, Bononcini went to Vienna, where together with his brother Antonio Maria, he worked mainly as an operatic composer until 1711. He continued this activity mainly in Rome until 1720, when he was called to London in order to work in the field of Italian opera at the Royal Academy of Music upon the invitation of Handel. After 1732, he traveled extensively on the continent, mainly to France, Lisbon, and Vienna, where he died. Known chiefly as an operatic composer in his lifetime, Bononcini is also remarkable for the composition of a number of fine chamber works.

BROSSARD, SÉBASTIEN DE (1655–1730)
First at Notre Dame in Paris and then canon at the cathedral of Meaux, de Brossard wrote a great deal of chamber music, but he is remembered ehiefly for his *Dictionnaire de musique* (1703), one of the first of its kind.

BUXTEHUDE, DIETRICH (1637–1707)
Born in Oldesloe (Holstein), Buxtehude spent his early life in Denmark and Sweden. In 1668 he was appointed organist and choirmaster at St. Mary's Church in Lübeck, one of the most important posts in German church music. At the same time he fulfilled the condition of marrying the daughter of his predecessor, Franz Tunder. Buxtehude had considerable influence on the organ style of Johann Sebastian Bach, who visited him in 1705.

CACCINI, GIULIO (1545–1618)
Caccini spent most of his life in the services of the Medici court in Florence. Since he was one of the more important members of the Camerata, he is credited with having written the first opera, together with Peri, without, however, ever attaining Peri's renown. The new age of music is indicated by the publication of his music in 1602, which bears the title *Le nuove musiche.*

CAVALLI, PIETRO FRANCESCO (1602–1676)
Successively singer, organist, and maestro di cappella at St. Mark's in Venice, Cavalli is known chiefly as an operatic composer, con-

tinuing the work of Monteverdi, under whose guidance he had embarked upon his career at St. Mark's.

CHAMBONNIÈRES, JACQUES CHAMPION DE (1602–1672)
Clavecinist under Louis XIII and Louis XIV and also at the courts of Sweden and Brandenburg, Chambonnières was one of the most famous harpsichord virtuosi of his days. His clavier works, a kind of extension of lutenist practices on the harpsichord, can be considered the point of departure of the French school of clavecinists.

CLÉRAMBAULT, LOUIS NICOLAS (1676–1749)
Organist at several Paris churches, most notably Saint Sulpice, Clérambault, in his organ works, is the last representative of the great French classical tradition. His clavecin works, however, are one of the departure points of Rococo music.

CORELLI, ARCANGELO (1653–1713)
After spending his student years in Bologna, Corelli settled, in 1685, in Rome as virtuoso violinist and composer. There Cardinal Ottoboni became his patron. He lived in the Cardinal's palace until his death. Occasional travels took him to the court of Modena and to Naples, where he met Alessandro Scarlatti. Corelli is remarkable not only for having established the ultimate Italian sonata form, but also for having laid the groundwork to orchestral writing in his concerti grossi.

COUPERIN, FRANÇOIS (1668–1733)
Like Bach, a member of a large family of musicians, Couperin, also known as "Le Grand," is the great master of the French Baroque and possibly also the founding father of some of the Rococo style. At first he was organist at Saint Gervais; then he became organist at the royal chapel of Louis XIV. Couperin's relation with the court never ceased. He was teacher of practically all the little princes and princesses and was made a chevalier of the Lateran Order. In the trio sonata, the suite, and, above all, the clavecin pieces, he was not only a pioneer but also an accomplished master. He also wrote the important theoretical work *L'Art de toucher le clavecin.*

DAQUIN, LOUIS CLAUDE (1694–1772)
At first, organist at Saint Paul (a post that he obtained after having defeated Rameau in the competition for it), Daquin was later appointed organist of the royal chapel. His fame rests on a variety of clavecin pieces, many of which have programmatic content.

DITTERSDORF, KARL DITTERS VON (1739–1799)
After having begun as a violinist in the cathedral and opera orchestras of Vienna, his native city, Dittersdorf went on a professional tour with Gluck in 1761. He then succeeded Michael Haydn as Kapellmeister to the Bishop of Grosswardein at Pressburg and later took up a similar post at Troppau with the Prince Bishop of Breslau, through whose influence he was knighted. On various guest appearances in Vienna he became acquainted with Emperor Joseph II, who thought highly of him. His last post was at the house of Count Stillfried in Bohemia. Dittersdorf gained much fame with his German *Singspiele,* most notably the light opera *Doktor und Apotheker,* but his symphonies and concerti are also fine examples of the rococo orchestral style.

FARINA, CARLO (ca. 1600–1640)
A violinist, who began his career at the court of Dresden and in Danzig, Farina returned to his native Italy. He was one of the first to exploit various effects on the violin, such as harmonics, pizzicato, *col legno,* and so on, and to create a picturesque imitation of extraneous impressions on this instrument in a rhapsodic form of solo sonata.

FASCH, JOHANN FRIEDRICH (1688–1758)
As a student of Kuhnau, Fasch wandered all over Germany until he settled in Gera as organist. Later, he entered the services of Count Morzin in Lucavec. Finally, he was court Kapellmeister in Zerbst. Fasch was invited to compete with Bach for the post of St. Thomas cantor, but refused to do so. Bach esteemed Fasch's orchestral music, which includes several suites.

FRANCK, MELCHOIR (1573–1639)
Known mainly as a composer of vocal quodlibets under the influence of folk music, the instrumental accompaniment of which was remarkable for its variety, Franck spent his life as Kapellmeister at the court of the Duke of Coburg.

FRESCOBALDI, GIROLAMO (1583–1643)
After having been an organist first in Rome and, later, for several years, in the Netherlands, Frescobaldi settled as organist of St. Peter's in Rome for the rest of his life, except for a period of six years during which he was organist to the court of the Medici in Florence. He was the leading keyboard composer of his time, and his influence on this type of work reached far beyond Italy, owing largely to the efforts of his pupil Froberger.

FROBERGER, JOHANN JACOB (1616–1667)
As a student of Frescobaldi, Froberger was court organist to Emperor Ferdinand III in Vienna. He also visited London, where he met Orlando Gibbons. The great amount of his keyboard writing as well as its quality make him an important representative of this style.

FUX, JOHANN JOSEPH (1660–1741)
Of Austrian peasant stock (Styria), Fux became one of Austria's most illustrious Baroque composers. He was Kapellmeister at St. Stephen's Cathedral in Vienna and court composer to Emperor Joseph I and Emperor Charles VI, for whose coronation in Bohemia he wrote his remarkable Baroque opera *Costanza e Fortezza.* He was a most versatile and prolific composer, and his strict polyphonic treatment has done much to give later Austrian music its contrapuntal tendency. His influence was still felt in the nineteenth century, when his famous treatise on counterpoint *Gradus ad Parnassum* was still in use as a basis of instruction.

GABRIELI, GIOVANNI (1557–1612)
After serving first as assistant to Lassus in Munich, Gabrieli returned to Venice, his birthplace, where he was to become successor to Merulo and, later, to his uncle Andrea Gabrieli as first organist

at St. Mark's. Influenced by the peculiar architecture of St. Mark's, he wrote for the specific acoustic conditions of this church a great number of choral-orchestral works full of echo effects and spaced-out sonorities. Through these works he influenced the development of Italian orchestral music, especially with regard to dynamics and the concerto.

GALILEI, VINCENZO (1520–1591)
The father of the great astronomer was an important member of the Florentine Camerata. He was among the first to develop the homophonic style, which he also defended in his theoretical writings, which were directed against his conservative teacher, Zarlino.

GALUPPI, BALDASSARE (1706–1785)
Beginning as a composer of operas for the Venetian opera house, Galuppi, who was born on Burano, an island near Venice, ultimately became maestro di cappella at St. Mark's. During his tenure he continued to write operas, which became so famous that he was invited to St. Petersburg. During the last twenty years of his life he was director of the Conservatorio degli Incurabili in Venice, which he raised to a high standard. Noted chiefly for his operatic output, which was considerable, he also deserves attention as an instrumental composer, mainly in the field of the concerto.

GAULTIER, JACQUES (first half of 17th century)
Having fled from France because of a duel, Gaultier settled in London and was appointed court lutenist. His fame as a virtuoso was so great that he was called to the Netherlands and to Madrid in his later years. His few extant compositions for the lute establish him as an important representative of this style.

GEMINIANI, FRANCESCO (1687–1762)
A student of Corelli, Geminiani went to England in 1714. There he became friendly with Handel. In 1733 he settled in Dublin. He returned to London in 1740, then went to Paris, where he remained until 1755. His last years were spent in Dublin. Geminiani was known in his lifetime mainly as a teacher. He raised the standard of violin playing in England to unbelievable heights. As a composer he concentrated on the concerto and sonata forms, in which

he accomplished considerable feats, although he never quite freed himself from the influence of Corelli.

GERVAISE, CLAUDE (early sixteenth century)
Violist at the court of King Francis I and King Henry II, Gervaise has come down to our day as composer of numerous instrumental dances, which were preserved because they were included in one of the earliest printed music publications by d'Attaignant (1529).

GESUALDO, CARLO, PRINCE OF VENOSA (1560–1613)
Of noble birth, Gesualdo was clearly a Renaissance personage. When he learned that his wife was unfaithful to him, he had her murdered. Gesualdo stayed mostly in Ferrara and Florence, where he probably was acquainted with the Camerata. His importance lies in the great expressiveness of the words and the far-reaching harmonic implications of his later madrigals. There is a marked veering toward the recitative style in these works, which leads one to believe that his association with Count Bardi may, indeed, have been very close.

GIBBONS, ORLANDO (1583–1625)
Born at Oxford, Gibbons grew up in Cambridge, where he entered the choir of King's College. Later, he became organist at the Royal Chapel and, finally, at Westminster Abbey. Perhaps he is the most English of the Tudor composers. His importance lies in his church music, but his instrumental fantasies and mainly his keyboard music show that he was a great master of the chamber style as well.

GLUCK, CHRISTOPH WILLIBALD RITTER VON (1714–1787)
Born in the Upper Palatinate, Gluck grew up in Bohemia and received his education in Prague. At the age of twenty-two he went to Vienna and from there to Milan, where he met Sammartini and where he wrote his first opera. In 1745 he went to London and met Handel. He also visited Rameau in Paris. After his London sojourn, he traveled widely all over Europe. For some time he was composer to the court of Francis I and Maria Theresia in Vienna. But his great reform of the opera, which he undertook in association with the poet Calzabigi, began only around 1758. Opera was

much under the influence of Lully and Rameau, and it was in France that he met opposition to his ideas mainly by the followers of the then highly popular opera composer Piccinni. Gluck finally retired to Vienna, where he heard with great pleasure *The Abduction from the Seraglio* by the young Mozart. Gluck is important chiefly as a great operatic composer and reformer. In his overtures he also shows a definite symphonic tendency, which did not pass unnoticed by the early Austrian symphonic school.

GRAUN, KARL HEINRICH (1704–1759)
When Kapellmeister at Wolfenbüttel–Brunswick, Graun met Frederick the Great, who engaged him as musical director for his orchestra at Rheinsberg. Later, Graun became the director of Frederick's opera house in Berlin, where he wrote many operas and a number of typical Rococo instrumental compositions.

GUILLEMAIN, LOUIS GABRIEL (1705–1770)
As violinist and composer attached to the royal chapel in Paris, Guillemain wrote a number of instrumental chamber works, typical of the late French Baroque style. At the age of sixty-five he committed suicide for an undisclosed reason.

HAMMERSCHMIDT, ANDREAS (1612–1675)
Of Austrian extraction, Hammerschmidt grew up in Saxony, where he became organist at Weesenstein Castle, Freiberg and Zittau. Many German chorale tunes were composed by him, but his importance lies in his expansion of the German instrumental suite.

HANDEL, GEORGE FRIDERIC (1685–1759)
In 1702, the year Handel entered the University of his native Halle to study law, he was appointed organist at the Cathedral. The year before, another law student, Georg Philipp Telemann, met Handel when passing through Halle on his way to Leipzig, and the two became lifelong friends. The following year Handel left the University, went to Hamburg, and, with the help of Johann Mattheson, obtained a post as violinist and harpsichordist at the opera. Here his first operas were produced. In 1706 he decided to spend some years in Italy, visiting Florence, Rome, Venice and Naples. In the course of these travels he met a number of Italian musicians, in-

cluding Corelli, Alessandro and Domenico Scarlatti and Marcello. During these years he wrote a number of Italian operas and cantatas. Upon his return to Germany in 1710, Handel was appointed Kapellmeister to the Elector Georg Ludwig of Hanover, but very soon thereafter obtained leave to visit London in the autumn of that year, from where he returned the following summer. In 1712 the Elector granted him another leave to visit England for a "reasonable time", but when Queen Anne died in 1714 and was succeeded by the Elector, who ascended the English throne as George I, Handel was still in England. This led to somewhat strained relations between the sovereign and his dilatory Kapellmeister, which, however, were soon smoothed out. Aside from occasional visits to the Continent, Handel remained in England for the rest of his life. Here he developed a new type of opera and created his great oratorios as well as his orchestral works, such as the *Concerti grossi,* the *Water Music* and the *Royal Fireworks Music.*

HASSE, JOHANN ADOLPH (1699–1783)
In the first rank among the early German operatic composers, Hasse had studied with Porpora and Alessandro Scarlatti in Naples. In Italy his fame was great, and he was appointed professor at the Scuola degli Incurabili in Venice. In 1731 he went to Dresden, where he was appointed director of the opera. He visited England, but did not wish to enter into rivalry with Handel. After the siege of Dresden in 1760, in the course of which he lost most of his fortune, Hasse and his wife, the celebrated prima donna Faustina Bordoni, went to Vienna, where he came into competition with Gluck. The last years of his life were spent in Venice.

HAYDN, FRANZ JOSEPH (1732–1809)
Of Austrian peasant stock, Haydn started his musical education at an early age as chorister at Vienna's St. Stephen's Cathedral, where his younger brother Michael joined him a few years later. Haydn's first job was that of accompanist to Porpora. He was later invited to Weinzierl, near Melk in Austria, to participate in performances of chamber music with a group of amateurs. It was there that his first instrumental compositions were written. After that he returned to Vienna. In 1759 he was appointed composer to Count Morzin at Lucavec in Bohemia. From there he went to the Esterhazy estab-

lishment (1761) as successor of Werner. In 1790, Haydn, by that time a famous man, moved to Vienna, where he was to remain for the rest of his life, except for short trips abroad, of which the two visits to London in 1790 and 1794 were most significant because they resulted in highly important works.

HEINICHEN, JOHANN DAVID (1683–1729)
A pupil of the St. Thomas School in Leipzig, Heinichen spent his early years as an opera composer in Italy. He settled in Dresden as opera director and, later, church conductor and remained there until his death. His theoretical work on the thorough bass (1711) was a standard for many years.

JENKINS, JOHN (1592–1678)
An English composer who resided most of his life with several noble English families, for whom he worked as musical tutor, Jenkins was one of the foremost composers of fantasies for viols.

KAUFMANN, GEORG FRIEDRICH (1679–1735)
A German organist, Kaufmann spent most of his life as conductor at the Court of Merseburg.

KERLL, JOHANN CASPAR (1627–1693)
After study in Italy, possibly as a fellow pupil of Froberger with Frescobaldi, Kerll returned to Germany and entered the service of the Bavarian elector. From 1677 to 1684, Kerll lived in Vienna, first, as organist at St. Stephen's Cathedral and, later, to the court. In 1685 he returned to Munich, where he died. He wrote many operas, but excelled in keyboard works, where his studies with Frescobaldi came to fruition.

KIRNBERGER, JOHANN PHILIPP (1721–1783)
A student of Bach from 1739 to 1741, Kirnberger, after travel in Poland, entered the service of Frederick the Great. Later, he became Kapellmeister at the establishment of Princess Amalie in Berlin, where he died. His theoretical works and reminiscences about Bach have kept his name alive.

KUHNAU, JOHANN (1660–1722)
From his first position, as cantor in Zittau, Kuhnau went to Leipzig in 1682, where he became organist and then cantor of St. Thomas in 1701. He was the predecessor of Bach in this post. Of his many works, the keyboard sonatas are of the highest importance.

KUSSER, JOHANN SIGISMUND (1660–1727)
An Austrian opera composer, who traveled successfully all over the continent, Kusser went to London in 1705 and later settled in Dublin. Besides his operas, he wrote a number of suites.

LECLAIR, JEAN MARIE (1697–1764)
The elder of two composing brothers, Leclair started out as ballet master in Turin, where he also composed several ballet interludes From there he went to Paris and became a member of the royal orchestra. After 1735 he lived in retirement in Paris, devoting his time to composition only. He was assassinated in Paris shortly after his return from an extensive trip to the Netherlands. His compositions are chiefly for solo violin, for which he evolved an extraordinary technique. Although influenced by the Italians, he developed his own typically French style, which makes him one of the leading composers of his nation.

LOCATELLI, PIETRO (1695–1764)
A pupil of Corelli, Locatelli became a foremost violin virtuoso. He traveled extensively on concert tours and finally settled in Amsterdam. In his violin works he demands unusual technical prowess; beyond that he shows great expressive powers as composer.

LULLY, JEAN-BAPTISTE (1632–1687)
Born in Italy, Lully was brought to France as a child. At an early age he became a member of the famous string band of Louis XIV. He was a favorite of the king, in whose service he remained until his death. Lully brought Italian influences to France and thus laid the groundwork to French Baroque music. In doing so, he was the first great master of the French style, which he developed on his own. His influence extended beyond that of Couperin. The high

point of his career was his collaboration with Molière and Quinault in operas, ballets, and plays, for which he wrote the music.

MARAIS, MARIN (1656–1728)
A member of the royal orchestra as violist and a pupil of Lully, Marais lived all his life in Paris. There he composed a great deal of chamber music, which is a forerunner of the typical French Rococo.

MARINI, BIAGIO (1597–1665)
An Italian violinist, Marini worked as maestro di cappella at Parma, at the court of the Duke of Bavaria in Munich, in Düsseldorf, and ultimately at the Accademia in Ferrara and at Santa Maria della Scala in Milan. He was one of the first to compose Italian concerted violin music.

MATTHESON, JOHANN (1681–1764)
Born in Hamburg, Mattheson wrote several operas for his native city, where he also became friendly with Handel. In 1715, he was appointed canon of the Hamburg Cathedral. His fame rests more on his books on music than on his compositions. His theoretical and practical writings give much documentation on the musical practices of his time. Most interesting of his great number of books is *Der vollkommene Kapellmeister*.

MERULO, CLAUDIO (1533–1604)
After serving as organist at St. Mark's in Venice for twenty years, Merulo went to Mantua and Parma, where he remained as organist of the ducal chapel for sixteen years and where he was knighted. Famous as a virtuoso, his keyboard pieces in the grand manner are fine examples of late Renaissance writing as it passes into the Baroque age.

MONN, GEORG MATTHIAS (1717–1750)
Organist at the Karlskirche in Vienna, Monn was one of the important composers of the Austrian school, which established the symphonic transition from the Rococo to the Classics.

MONTEVERDI, CLAUDIO (1567–1643)
The greatest of the early Baroque composers, Monteverdi grew up in Cremona, then entered the service of the ducal court in Mantua. In 1613, he was appointed maestro di cappella at St. Mark's in Venice, where he died. Starting out as a typical Renaissance composer, Monteverdi underwent many stylistic changes, into which he absorbed the ideas of the Camerata. He was an innovator only in the sense that in him the new ideas reached complete mastery. Not only in the operas, but also in the development of instrumental accompaniment to the madrigals, which with him took a highly dramatic form, did his influence become decisive.

MOZART, (JOHANN GEORG) LEOPOLD (1719–1787)
The father of the great Wolfgang originally came from Augsburg. He studied at Salzburg, where he first became a member of the Canon's orchestra and, later, of that of the Archbishop. He finally was made composer and second Kapellmeister at the latter's establishment. Of his numerous compositions, the instrumental works are of remarkable quality.

MOZART, WOLFGANG AMADEUS (1756–1791)
As an infant prodigy, young Mozart traveled extensively. Of these travels, those to England, where he met the "London Bach," and Italy were important because they afforded the child the opportunity to absorb many important influences and to develop a cosmopolitan view. It is significant that, because of this, Mozart freed himself from the bondage of the service at Salzburg and settled as a free-lance musician in Vienna. He was the first of the Rococo composers who undertook the important step from feudal servant to freely creating artist, a phenomenon which only became universal with Beethoven. It is this forward looking combined with being rooted in the past that gives Mozart's music its universal, immortal character.

MUFFAT, GEORG (1645–1704)
After extensive studies in Paris, Muffat became organist at the Cathedral of Strasbourg. Later he accepted the post of an organist in Salzburg and finally that of a Kapellmeister to the Bishop of Pas-

sau. His student years in Paris and some trips to Italy stood him in good stead, for they inspired him to combine the characteristic stylistic elements of these two countries with his own Germanic background. This combination manifests itself most in his outstanding instrumental collection, *Auserlesene mit Ernst und Lust gemengte Instrumental Musik,* of which even the title is a combination of attitudes of both the northern and southern countries.

MUNDY, JOHN (?–1630)
An English organist at Eton college and, later, at St. George's Chapel in Windsor, Mundy wrote madrigals and some church music, but he is best known for his keyboard pieces, some of which are in the *Fitzwilliam Virginal Book.*

MYSLIVECEK, JOSEPH (1737–1781)
After initial studies in his native Bohemia, Myslivecek went to Italy, where he gained a measure of success with his operas. He was then invited to Munich where he became seriously afflicted with venereal disease. Mozart visited him in the hospital. Still ill, he went to Italy, where he was able to produce a few more operas with great success. He lived in Rome, where he was highly esteemed, but in his later days he was definitely on the downgrade. He finally died, a pauper, in Rome. Myslivecek has written charming instrumental pieces, of which Mozart said, "they are bound to please, not difficult and very effective."

PERGOLESI, GIOVANNI BATTISTA (1710–1736)
The son of a shoemaker, probably afflicted with tuberculosis all his life, this tragic genius is the most important link outside France between the Baroque and the Rococo. Pergolesi studied at Naples, where he was also the deputy of the official maestro di cappella of the city. A mass that he composed was performed with great success in Rome. Of his operas, mainly the buffo works found large acceptance. In addition to these and some very valuable sacred music, his instrumental compositions are the ones that establish his fame for future times.

PERI, JACOPO (1561–1633)
Peri, the Roman-born offspring of a noble family of Florence, was an important member of the Camerata. Together with Caccini, he wrote the first opera and a number of interludes for festive occasions. He was one of the first to be engaged in extensive writing of monodic chamber music and songs with instrumental accompaniment. Most of his life was spent in Florence, where he died.

PEUERL, PAUL (ca. 1575–ca. 1628)
An Austrian composer from Styria Peuerl combined several dances in variation form into orchestral suites.

PEZEL, JOHANN CHRISTOPH (1639–1694)
As *Stadtpfeifer,* first in Leipzig and then in Bautzen, Pezel (also known as Petzold) wrote a great number of instrumental pieces, which he performed on his posts on various occasions.

PHILIPS, PETER (between 1560 and 1570–between 1633 and 1640)
Born in England, Philips traveled probably to Italy and spent a great deal of his time in Antwerp. He was known principally as a vocal composer (madrigals and motets). His harpsichord pieces, collected in the *Fitzwilliam Virginal Book,* show more of the continental influence than typically English traits.

PORPORA, NICOLA ANTONIO (1686–1766)
His early operas were produced in his native Naples, where he was engaged as maestro at the Conservatory. Porpora visited Vienna, where his operas enjoyed great popularity. He probably succeeded Heinichen in Dresden. In London he was the rival of Handel between 1733 and 1736. After this date he returned to Italy, going first to Venice and later to Naples. He then returned to Dresden as Kapellmeister and left this post in 1752 for Vienna. The last eight years of his life were spent in Naples. During his lifetime, he was a very popular opera composer. His violin sonatas are still of interest today, and some of his instrumental music is quite unjustly neglected.

POSSENTI, PELLEGRINO (beginning of 17th century)
Although chiefly an Italian vocal composer, Possenti produced *Concentus armonici*, a collection of instrumental pieces, which is interesting as an early sample of instrumental style.

PRAETORIUS, MICHAEL (1571–1621)
Kapellmeister at Lüneburg, then with the Duke of Brunswick in Wolfenbüttel, Praetorius is important as the author of *Syntagma Musicum*, a theoretical treatise published in 1615. It is a highly valuable source for the music of that time.

PURCELL, HENRY (1659–1695)
The great genius of English music was the successor of John Blow as organist at Westminster Abbey. Later on, he became the organist of the Chapel Royal. He is the outstanding English Baroque composer. His typical English style is manifested best in his numerous anthems and in the incidental music to various plays. There are also a great many instrumental compositions and keyboard pieces, which are on a high level. His *Dido and Aeneas* was the first opera in English.

QUANTZ, JOHANN JOACHIM (1697–1773)
Well-known as a flautist, Quantz traveled widely. In Italy he met Hasse and Scarlatti, and after visiting London and Paris, he settled as Kammermusikus in Berlin in the services of Frederick the Great, his former pupil on the flute. His compositions are mainly for the flute, for which he wrote idiomatically and quite ingeniously. We know much about Rococo practices of ornamentation from his theoretical writings, of which the "Essay of an Instruction how to Play the Transverse Flute" has become a standard work.

RAMEAU, JEAN-PHILIPPE (1683–1764)
After initial studies in Italy, Rameau became music master in Avignon and Clermont-Ferrand. He then worked briefly as organist in Paris, after which he returned to Dijon, his birthplace, to succeed his father in the post of organist. He left there again for Clermont-Ferrand, where he lived for seven years. Only when he was in his forties could he settle in Paris. There he began to write

his operas, which eventually spread his fame. However, when Pergolesi's *La serva padrona* was performed in Paris, the Encyclopedists vociferously preferred it to Rameau's works, and the discussion of Italian versus French style and of old versus new flared up once again. This "guerre des bouffons" was eventually forgotten and today, from an historical angle, it is easy to see that both Pergolesi and Rameau guided the Baroque into the Rococo style. In addition to his quite novel operas and excellent keyboard works, Rameau wrote also the basic theoretical work on tonal harmony, *Traité de l'harmonie.*

ROSENMÜLLER, JOHANN (1619–1684)
After studying at Leipzig's St. Thomas School, Rosenmüller became cantor there and organist at St. Nicholas. However, midway in his career, he was jailed for a grave moral offense. Eventually he escaped to Hamburg, went on to Venice, and was finally called as Kapellmeister to the court of the Duke of Brunswick in Wolfenbüttel, where he settled for the rest of his life. Rosenmüller is the foremost of the early German instrumental composers. Undoubtedly, the development of his style owes much to Italian music, with which he must have been very familiar through his stay in Venice, where he got to know much of Gabrieli's music.

ROSSI, SALOMONE (1570–1630)
Descendant of an Italian-Jewish family, Rossi added to his name "Ebreo.' He served as musician at the Mantua court of the Gonzaga dukes and was held in such esteem that he was permitted to forgo the yellow badge of the Jews. After the death of his patron, however, he had to flee from Mantua with the other Jews. In all probability he settled in Venice. Rossi composed largely for the Jewish religious service, but he wrote a great deal of chamber music as well. His is the first complete trio sonata (1607) to reach the world in printed form.

SAMMARTINI, GIOVANNI BATTISTA (1698–1775)
A Milanese composer whose influence on the instrumental compositions of his time was great, Sammartini was, for a while, the teacher of Gluck. Mozart also visited him. In his instrumental works, Sammartini experimented in contracting the form which

eventually helped to determine the future structure of the string quartet and symphony.

SCARLATTI, (PIETRO) ALESSANDRO GASPARE (1660–1725)
Probably a pupil of Carissimi, Scarlatti wrote operas for the Roman stage. He was appointed maestro di cappella of the royal chapel in Naples in 1684. Except for seven years (from 1702 to 1709), which he spent as maestro di cappella at Santa Maria Maggiore in Rome and for his patron, the Cardinal Ottoboni, he lived in Naples. Scarlatti was the commanding figure in Italian opera in his time. He was visited by many important European composers and for a while was the teacher of Hasse. His opera overtures were a decisive influence in the development of instrumental music.

SCARLATTI, (GIUSEPPE) DOMENICO (1685–1757)
Son and also student of Alessandro Scarlatti, Domenico went briefly to Florence and thence to Venice. There he studied with Gasparini and met Handel. In 1709, he settled in Rome where he accepted successively various posts with the Queen of Poland, the Portuguese ambassador, and at the Vatican. He entered the service of the royal chapel in Lisbon in the 1720's, but returned to Italy a few years later. Finally around 1729, at the age of forty-four, he settled in Madrid. His operas and oratorios were all written in and for Italy. His keyboard work, however, which is the all-important part of his output, was created in Spain. These works established a definite harmonic style and introduced the dual theme, the important forerunner of the Rococo and Classical sonata.

SCHEIDT, SAMUEL (1587–1654)
A pupil of Sweelinck, Scheidt spent all his life as organist of the Moritzkirche and as Kapellmeister to the Margrave of Brandenburg, then governing Halle, his native city. He is important for the development of German organ music, especially in its relation to the chorale, and for being among the first to develop the practice of thorough bass.

SCHEIN, JOHANN HERMANN (1586–1630)
From 1615 until his death, Schein was cantor at the St. Thomas School in Leipzig. As a composer he developed the German instrumental style under the influence of Viadana, giving the instruments a far more interesting melodic line than was generally known then in Germany.

SCHÜTZ, HEINRICH (1558–1672)
At an early age Schütz visited Venice, where he worked under the tutelage of Gabrieli. He returned to Germany and took up a post in Dresden. Most of his life was spent there, but because of the vicissitudes of the Thirty Years War, he was obliged to leave Dresden several times. He spent the years of his absence from Dresden at the courts of Copenhagen and Hanover. Schütz has often been called the German Monteverdi. A composer of great genius, he certainly is the most influential force in early German Baroque. Special importance attaches to the fact that he brought the influence of Gabrieli and the Venetian school into Germany. It was he who wrote the first German opera, *Daphne*, subsequently lost in a fire.

SOLER, ANTONIO (1729–1783)
A Spanish composer who became a monk of the Order of St. Jerome, Soler was organist and choirmaster of the royal monastery at the Escorial and taught music to the members of the Spanish royal family. He probably was a pupil of Domenico Scarlatti, whose influence is reflected in his keyboard music, which is for both organ and harpsichord.

STAMITZ, JOHANN (1717–1757)
Of Styrian extraction, Stamitz was born and educated in Bohemia. He was well-known as a virtuoso on various string instruments and became a member of the Mannheim Orchestra in 1741 and its Kapellmeister in 1745. From Mannheim he visited Paris. He brought the Mannheim Orchestra to a very high level, teaching it a new style of playing, necessitated by the novel instrumental music, for the creation of which, under Italian influence, he was partly re-

sponsible. His are the first important German symphonies that show the inception of the cyclical form.

STAMITZ, KARL (PHILIPP) (1745–1801)
Karl Stamitz studied with his father and Franz Xaver Richter, another important composer of the Mannheim school. He was well-known as a violin virtuoso and traveled widely to such cities as Paris, London, and St. Petersburg. In 1794 he became leading violinist in Jena, where he settled and finally died. His instrumental works are an elaboration on the cyclical principle instituted by his father.

STARZER, JOSEF (ca. 1726–1787)
As violinist, Starzer was engaged by the Vienna court chapel and, later, by the Russian court in St. Petersburg. From there he returned to his Vienna post. He wrote numerous ballets, into which he gradually introduced new symphonic form.

SÜSSMAYR, FRANZ XAVER (1766–1803)
Süssmayr was a pupil of Salieri and Mozart, to whom he became closely attached. His compositions show Mozart's influence to a marked degree. His fame lies in the fact that he completed Mozart's *Requiem* with such exceptional empathy with Mozart's style that it has come to us as a completely Mozartean work.

SWEELINCK, JAN PIETERSZOON (1562–1621)
The famous Dutch organ composer Sweelinck lived all his life in Amsterdam and never left the Netherlands. Of the important Netherlands period he was the last great composer. He was also the first to establish a new and more modern harmonic base in his keyboard works.

TARTINI, GIUSEPPE (1692–1770)
A famous violin virtuoso, Tartini's early years were turbulent because of a marriage that incurred the wrath of his father. He fled Padua and spent some years in Ancona and Assisi. In 1721 he returned to Padua where he worked as violinist in the Basilica di Sant' Antonio. From 1723 to 1725 he was in Prague as a conductor of Count Kinski's orchestra. Despite his fantastic success there, he

returned to Padua, where he founded a famous school for violinists. From there he also undertook a number of concert tours, but basically he remained in Padua until his death. As a composer he extended the technical prerequisites of the violin, but his works stand decidedly under the influence of Corelli.

TELEMANN, GEORG PHILIPP (1681–1767)
In his youth Telemann held various posts, but, in 1721, he settled in Hamburg as music director of the Johanneum and the five principal churches of the city, where he remained until his death. A highly prolific composer, he was well acquainted with the works of Lully and Campra, whose influence is noticeable in his mixing of French and German styles. Because of this French influence, Telemann occupies the dual position of one of the last Baroque composers and one of the earliest German Rococo composers.

TORELLI, GIUSEPPE (1658–1709)
Well-known as a violinist, Torelli spent the first part of his life in Bologna and the second part at the court of the Margrave of Brandenburg-Ansbach. Although the earlier contention that Torelli was the inventor of the concerto form cannot be maintained, his concerti grossi have contributed substantially to the advancement of this form.

TUNDER, FRANZ (1614–1667)
As a student of Frescobaldi, Tunder became the organist at St. Mary's Church in Lübeck, a post that he held until his death and in which he was succeeded by his son-in-law Buxtehude. As a composer, he brought some of Frescobaldi's influence to bear on the more austere northern organ chorale music. He also enlarged the instrumental ensembles in St. Mary's Church. This ensemble enabled him to give his series of famous "Abendmusiken," which influenced much of the later German cantata writing.

TÜRK, DANIEL GOTTLOB (1756–1813)
First, cantor, then, music director at the University at Halle, Türk, a pupil of Hiller in composition, was known as a writer on musical subjects which illuminate the practices of his times.

VALENTINI, GIOVANNI (?–1649)
An Italian organist who spent most of his life as imperial court organist to Emperor Ferdinand II in Vienna. Valenti's sonatas for strings are early instrumental samples.

VERACINI, FRANCESCO MARIA (1690–1750)
One of the foremost violin virtuosi of his day, Veracini traveled widely. He was in England, stayed for a while in Dresden, went to Prague, and returned to London. He wrote a number of interesting violin works, of which the concerti are the best.

VIADANA (1564–1645)
The Italian composer Lodovico Grossi, who came to be known as Viadana, the name of his birthplace, was maestro di cappella at the Cathedral of Mantua, where Monteverdi met him. He became a Franciscan monk in 1596, and his last post was that of organist at the Cathedral of Fano. He then retired to the Franciscan monastery at Gualtieri, where he died. He is credited with having established the method of the basso continuo in his *Concerti ecclesiastici*. Whether he was really the inventor of the thorough bass has never been firmly established. Nevertheless, his use of this technique influenced Peri, Caccini, Cavalieri, and even Monteverdi.

VISÉE, ROBERT DE (ca. 1650–ca. 1725)
Guitarist to the dauphin and then to the king, Visée wrote for lute, theorbo, and guitar. It is in the compositions for the last instrument that he is representative of the French style.

VITALI, GIOVANNI BATTISTA (1644–1692)
Starting as violist at the church of San Petronio in Bologna, Vitali advanced to maestro di cappella at the court of Modena. He is one of the first to experiment in the instrumental form of the Italian chamber sonata, writing both *sonate da chiesa* and *sonate da camera*.

VIVALDI, ANTONIO (1678–1741)
Son of a violinist at St. Mark's in Venice, where he was born, Vivaldi took minor orders at an early age and, because of his red hair,

was nicknamed the "red priest." He taught at the Conservatory, but while there took repeated leaves of absence, during which he went to the court at Mantua and took an extended trip through Germany. Vivaldi was recognized as an important composer during his lifetime, when Bach was much impressed by his music. Essentially he is a Baroque composer who leans toward the harmonic style and shows great preoccupation with structure arising from the harmonic concertato style. Although the recent years have brought about a renaissance of Vivaldi's music, the surface has only been skimmed, with many manuscript scores as yet not even deciphered. On a rough count, Vivaldi can be credited with the creation of forty-four operas, more than two dozen secular cantatas, about two and a half dozen sacred vocal works, close to five hundred concerti, about six dozens of chamber sonatas, and two dozen symphonies.

WAGENSEIL, GEORG CHRISTOPH (1715–1777)
A pupil of Fux, upon whose recommendation he received the post of court composer, which he retained to his death, Wagenseil was an important member of the Austrian school which developed early symphonic writing.

WALTHER, JOHANN GOTTFRIED (1684–1748)
A relative of Bach and his intimate during the Weimar days, Walther was organist at Erfurt, then at Weimar where, eventually, he became Hofmusicus. He wrote many keyboard compositions, mostly on chorales, but he is famous for his *Musikalisches Lexikon* (1732), the first work to combine biographical data with musical subject matter.

WERCKMEISTER, ANDREAS (1645–1706)
The importance of Werckmeister, organist at Hasselfelde, Quedlinburg, and, finally, Halberstadt, where he died, lies in his theoretical writings, which occupy themselves with problems of acoustics and temperament. His book *Musikalische Temperatur* (1691) exercised a certain influence on the tuning in equal temperament.

ZARLINO, GIOSEFFO (1517–1590)
Although appointed maestro di cappella at St. Mark's in Venice in 1565, Zarlino, who had taken minor orders and throughout his life

exercised clerical functions, was primarily a theoretician. He was the conservative element when the new theories of the Camerata developed, and Galilei, who had been his pupil, attacked him violently in two essays, of which the second, "Dialogo della musica antica e della moderna" (1581; second enlarged edition 1602) established the new, if somewhat amateurish, standpoint of monodic composers. Zarlino's line of counterargument was followed up after his death by Artusi.

Notes on Historical Instruments Used in These Recordings

Harpsichord

This instrument is in the possession of Hilde Langfort. It was built in 1958–59 by Sperrhake in Passau, Germany, under the direction of Miss Langfort, who tried to achieve an optimum combination of the sound of various outstanding historical instruments, which it imitates in measurement and design.

Clavichord

In the possession of Hans Kann, this instrument was built in 1963 by Neupert, in exact imitation of an instrument by Hubert, which is now exhibited in a museum in Munich. The instrument comprises five octaves.

Organ positive

In the possession of Josef Mertin, the organ was built in 1718 by Gottlieb Hencke, a Westphalian, who had his workshop in Vienna next to the workshops of several other keyboard instrument builders, such as Zimmermann and Walter. It was built for the Schwarzspanier monastery in Vienna. When the monastery was closed, because of an edict issued by Emperor Josef II, the organ was transferred to the parish of St. Augustin and, later on, to the Diozesanmuseum, Vienna, where it was acquired by Mr. Mertin in 1930. Mr. Mertin is one of Europe's foremost organ builders, a specialist in the restoration of valuable Baroque instruments.

Virginal

This virginal is a copy of a seventeenth-century instrument, which carries the inscription "Ioannes et Andreas Ruckers fecerunt, 1604," built by Kurt Wittmayer, Gartenberg, in 1965.

In order to achieve a completely authentic sound, it is unavoidable that on our historical instruments, including the copies, a certain amount of noise is heard together with the performance.